Greek Tragedy, Education, and Theatre Practices in the UK Classics Ecology

Through a series of case studies, this book explores the interrelations among Greek tragedy, theatre practices, and education in the United Kingdom. This is situated within what the volume proposes as 'the Classics ecology'.

The term 'ecology', frequently used in Theatre Studies, understands Classics as a field of cultural production dependent on shared knowledge circulated via formal and informal networks, which operate on the basis of mutually beneficial exchange. Productions of Greek tragedy may be influenced by members of the team studying Classics subjects at school or university, or reading popular works of Classical scholarship, or else by working with an academic consultant. All of these have some degree of connection to academic Classics, albeit filtered through different lenses, creating a network of mutual influence and benefit (the ecology). In this way, theatrical productions of Greek drama may, in the long term, influence Classics as an academic discipline, and certainly contribute to attesting to the relevance of Classics in the modern world. The chapters in this volume include contributions by both theatre makers and academics, whose backgrounds vary between Theatre Studies and Classics. They comprise a variety of case studies and approaches, exploring the dissemination of knowledge about the ancient world through projects that engage with Greek tragedy, theories and practices of theatre making through the chorus, and practical relationships between scholars and theatre makers. By understanding the staging of Greek tragedy in the United Kingdom today as being part of the Classics ecology, the book examines practices and processes as key areas in which the value of engaging with the ancient past is (re)negotiated.

This book is primarily suitable for students and scholars working in Classical Reception and Theatre Studies who are interested in the reception history of Greek tragedy and the intersection of the two fields. It is also of use to more general Classics and Theatre Studies audiences, especially those engaged with current debates around 'saving Classics' and those interested in a structural, systemic approach to the intersection between theatre, culture, and class.

David Bullen is Lecturer in Drama and Theatre at Royal Holloway, University of London, as well as a director, writer, and dramaturg. Both his research and practice explore politicised re-uses of traditional narratives and forms, especially feminist, queer, and ecocritical adaptations of Greek myth and tragedy.

Christine Plastow is Lecturer in Classical Studies at the Open University. Her research has two strands: practice-as-research work with ancient myth exploring its value and potential for modern audiences, and social-historical, legal, and rhetorical investigations of Greek oratory, particularly forensic oratory from fourth-century Athens.

Classics In and Out of the Academy: Classical Pedagogy in the Twenty-First Century
Edited by Fiona McHardy and Nancy Sorkin Rabinowitz

This series of short volumes explores the ways in which the study of antiquity can enrich the lives of diverse populations in the twenty-first century. The series covers two distinct, but interrelated topics: 1) ways in which classicists can engage new audiences within the profession by embedding inclusivity and diversity in school and university teaching practices, curricula, and assessments, and 2) the relevance of Classics to learners from the most marginalized social strata (e.g. the incarcerated, refugees, those suffering from mental illness).

Classics and Prison Education in the US
Edited by Emilio Capettini and Nancy Sorkin Rabinowitz

Classics at Primary School
A Tool for Social Justice
Evelien Bracke

Expanding Classics
Practitioner Perspectives from Museums and Schools
Edited by Arlene Holmes-Henderson

Diversity and the Study of Antiquity in Higher Education
Perspectives from North America and Europe
Edited by Daniel Libatique and Fiona McHardy

Greek Tragedy, Education, and Theatre Practices in the UK
Classics Ecology
Edited by David Bullen and Christine Plastow

Greek Tragedy, Education, and Theatre Practices in the UK Classics Ecology

Edited by David Bullen and Christine Plastow

LONDON AND NEW YORK

First published 2024
by Routledge
4 Park Square, Milton Park, Abingdon, Oxon OX14 4RN

and by Routledge
605 Third Avenue, New York, NY 10158

Routledge is an imprint of the Taylor & Francis Group, an informa business

© 2024 selection and editorial matter, David Bullen and Christine Plastow; individual chapters, the contributors

The right of David Bullen and Christine Plastow to be identified as the authors of the editorial material, and of the authors for their individual chapters, has been asserted in accordance with sections 77 and 78 of the Copyright, Designs and Patents Act 1988.

All rights reserved. No part of this book may be reprinted or reproduced or utilised in any form or by any electronic, mechanical, or other means, now known or hereafter invented, including photocopying and recording, or in any information storage or retrieval system, without permission in writing from the publishers.

Trademark notice: Product or corporate names may be trademarks or registered trademarks, and are used only for identification and explanation without intent to infringe.

British Library Cataloguing-in-Publication Data
A catalogue record for this book is available from the British Library

Library of Congress Cataloging-in-Publication Data
Names: Bullen, David (Lecturer in drama and theater), editor. | Plastow, Christine, editor.
Title: Greek tragedy, education, and theatre practices in the UK classics ecology / edited by David Bullen and Christine Plastow.
Description: Abingdon, Oxon ; New York, NY : Routledge, 2024. | Series: Classics in and out of the academy | Includes bibliographical references and index.
Identifiers: LCCN 2024004413 (print) | LCCN 2024004414 (ebook) | ISBN 9781032256788 (hardback) | ISBN 9781032256795 (paperback) | ISBN 9781003284536 (ebook)
Subjects: LCSH: Greek drama--Modern presentation. | Greek drama (Tragedy)--Appreciation--Great Britain. | Greek drama (Tragedy)--Study and teaching--Great Britain. | Classical literature--Appreciation.
Classification: LCC PA3238 .G748 2024 (print) | LCC PA3238 (ebook) | DDC 882.0071/041--dc23/eng/20240508
LC record available at https://lccn.loc.gov/2024004413
LC ebook record available at https://lccn.loc.gov/2024004414

ISBN: 978-1-032-25678-8 (hbk)
ISBN: 978-1-032-25679-5 (pbk)
ISBN: 978-1-003-28453-6 (ebk)

DOI: 10.4324/b22844

Typeset in Times New Roman
by KnowledgeWorks Global Ltd.

For collaborators, past, present, and future.

Contents

Acknowledgements	*xi*
List of Contributors	*xii*
List of Figures	*xiv*

1 **Introducing the Classics Ecology**   1
CHRISTINE PLASTOW AND DAVID BULLEN

PART I
Mediating Knowledge(s)   17

2 **Towards Co-creation: Roles of Classics Academics in Modern Productions of Greek Tragedy**   19
CHRISTINE PLASTOW

3 **Between Actors and Archons: Mediating Knowledges of Greek Tragedy in/as Performance**   31
DAVID BULLEN

4 **The King's Greek Play and the Classics Ecology**   42
PETER SWALLOW

PART II
Choral Practice and Participation   55

5 **Greek Tragedy in the Drama Studio: Lecoq, Agonism, and the Politics of Choral Pedagogy**   57
STEPHE HARROP

6 The Pedagogic Value of Participating in a Chorus 70
HELEN EASTMAN AND ALEX SILVERMAN

7 Community Choruses and the Value of Participation in
Contemporary Productions in the United Kingdom 84
SARAH WESTON

PART III
Academics and/as Practitioners 97

8 Sheffest: Bringing Ancient Greek Theatre to Sheffield 99
LOTTIE PARKYN

9 Making Theatre Out of Fragments 113
LAURA SWIFT

Index *126*

Acknowledgements

The editors would like to thank the following for their help and support in the creation of this volume: Nancy Rabinowitz, Fiona McHardy, Marcia Adams, Amy Davis-Poynter, Mathura Umachandran, Marchella Ward, Fiona Macintosh, Tamsin Shasha, Lucy Ruddiman, Mark Katz, E-J Graham, Emma Bridges, Jasmine Hunter Evans, Ursula Rothe, James Robson, Helen Nicholson, Emma Cox, Chris Megson, Liz Schafer, Rebecca McCutcheon, María Estrada-Fuentes, Will Shüler, Dan Rebellato, Prarthana Purkayastha, Roberta Mock, Efi Spentzou, and all of our patient, game contributors. We would like to add special thanks to our partners, Tom and Alex, whose daily support enabled this volume to reach publication.

Contributors

Helen Eastman is a writer, director, and translator, with a PhD in Classics. She is Artistic Director and CEO of Creation Theatre, Artistic Associate of the APGRD at Oxford University and Visiting Lecturer in Theatre and Creative Writing at Westminster University. She founded Live Canon and co-founded Barefaced Greek.

Stephe Harrop is Associate Professor of Drama at Liverpool Hope University. Her research and teaching centres upon Greek tragedy and classical receptions, performer training, and contemporary storytelling practices. She co-authored *Greek Tragedy and the Contemporary Actor* (Palgrave 2018), and her most recent monograph is *Contemporary Storytelling Performance* (Routledge 2023).

Lottie Parkyn is the Director for Research and Partnerships at The University of Notre Dame London Global Gateway, where she teaches classes on Greek tragedy and reception. Her research explores 'lost' stories/voices of the ancient past and she is passionate about supporting activities for non-academic audiences.

Alex Silverman is an award-winning musician and a classicist. As a composer and musical director specialising in stage works, he has worked with many of the United Kingdom's major playhouses. Alex has been composer and music director for the Cambridge Greek Play since 2010 and contributes to performance and research projects at the APGRD in Oxford.

Peter Swallow is a Research Fellow at Durham University. He previously worked at KCL and Goldsmiths. He is the author of *Aristophanes in Britain* (OUP 2023) and sits on the Classical Association Teaching Board. He also works with the Advocating Classics Education project to expand access to Classics in schools.

Laura Swift is Associate Professor of Classics at the University of Oxford, and Tutorial Fellow at Magdalen College. Her research focuses on Greek tragedy, chorality, and lyric poetry, and she has recently been working with theatre practitioners on how to stage fragmentary texts as a contemporary art form.

Sarah Weston is Lecturer in Theatre Studies at the University of Manchester. Her research explores socially engaged performance practice, with interests in areas such as community plays, voice, and performance training. She also works as a theatre practitioner, co-running Salford Community Theatre.

Figures

6.1 The chorus of *Antigone* find themselves in formation at the archaeological site of Oiniades. Photograph: Michael Garrett   74
6.2 The masked *Oedipus* chorus dance on their chairs. Images captured by performers from the Live Canon ensemble   76
6.3 Janis Sarra's lecture on corporate financial responsibility is drowned out by a dissenting chorus. Photograph: Michael Garrett   79
9.1 In the 2017 Ovalhouse showing, performers experimented with using shapes on the OHP to represent 'realistic papyrology'. Artists: Bella Heesom and Tom Espiner. Photograph: Richard Wylie   121
9.2 During puppetry workshops in 2020, the creative team experimented with moving and manipulating fragments of real (modern) papyri until finally the image of a king becomes clear. Photograph: Russell Bender   121

1 Introducing the Classics Ecology

Christine Plastow and David Bullen

This volume is concerned with (at least) two things: knowledge about, and study of, the ancient Greek and Roman worlds, their languages, literature, history, archaeology, and reception; and the discipline of Classics. They are not direct equivalents. Classics is an academic discipline concerned with the study of the ancient Greek and Roman worlds; European in origin, it has historically been concerned with identifying Greece and Rome as the foundation of European civilisation—a foundation imagined as literate, refined, and supremely powerful. This identification has (among other effects) provided a narrative to support a common European (and subsequently 'Western') identity; in particular, European imperialist projects have capitalised on a sense of inheritance from the ancient world to shore up claims of superiority.[1] The discipline was traditionally concerned with philology, initially focusing on texts in Latin, then also in Greek, almost exclusively written by elite men. In the British context—in which these factors crystallised in particular ways—Classics has historically been the preserve of the white upper class; it has been associated with a particular kind of elite education that idealises progression through certain private schools and Oxbridge and into high-profile jobs. In the 21st century, the paradigm of this ideal is (disgraced) former UK Prime Minister Boris Johnson (to whom we return later). Even as Classics expanded beyond literature to consider history and archaeology, the subject matter has been narrow in scope: the societies of ancient Greece and Rome were generally patriarchal, engaged in enslavement, and economically unequal, and the interests of the dominant group that has historically studied this ancient world have not often, and not until relatively recently, extended beyond this limited range of experiences. This narrow focus and sense of elitism is signalled by the very name of the subject, 'Classics', which both names the literary texts of ancient Greece and Rome as superior and foundational and aligns the academic discipline with the subject matter ('the' Classics). Certainly, the ancient world is worth studying, and the modern subject of Classics is not simplistically or uniformly 'bad' (we, the authors, would be hypocrites if we were to take such a position).[2] But the naming-and-claiming of certain knowledge

DOI: 10.4324/b22844-1

invoked by the term 'Classics' interests us, and in this introduction, we outline an approach to thinking about the term's tensions in productive ways.

Classics is, perhaps, on the verge of extinction. Classics departments in universities (not only in the United Kingdom) are being defunded and shut down. This follows decreasing provision of Classics subjects in schools. In 2021, Stephen Hunt and Arlene Holmes-Henderson showed that access to Classics-related subjects is particularly limited outside of London and the Southeast. Data in 2019 showed numbers of both students and staff in Classics at universities were declining (Marshall); this has continued, with departmental closures including Archaeology at Sheffield in 2021 and Classics at Roehampton in 2022. The situation reflects the wider agenda of the Conservative government, which has cut funding to and sought to impose restrictions on student numbers for many arts and humanities disciplines, prioritising a focus on STEM subjects. Other disciplines have also faced departmental closures, though arguably with less outcry than seems to arise in the case of Classics.[3]

But while neoliberal forces contribute to driving Classics to extinction, its decline is also arguably in many ways a result of natural selection. In recent years, the dominance of Classics as a discipline has been challenged by its elite associations, both in subject matter and access. The ways in which the discipline has upheld inequality have led some researchers to call for Classics to come to an end; see, for example, the work of Dan-el Padilla Peralta (summarised in Poser). Others have attempted to open up and modernise the discipline: by expanding curricula to consider, for example, areas outside of the Greek and Roman worlds such as ancient Asia and Africa, or to seek evidence for gender diversity in ancient contexts, or the lives of ancient enslaved people; by making efforts to decolonise the discipline in terms of its operation, for example by expanding reading lists to contain works by scholars from global majority backgrounds; and, most crucially, by removing historic ancient language requirements for applicants to university courses. Even these moderate (and often only minimally inclusive) attempts at change have been decried by conservative classicists and commentators as 'destabilisation of the discipline' (Butterfield) and even the 'toxic substitution of identity politics for humanistic learning' ('Decline & Fall: Classics Edition'). Nevertheless, the point is clear: like species that fail to adapt to their changing environment, it may be that Classics will not survive.

The other option is evolution: a radical new discipline for the study of the ancient Greek and Roman worlds—such as that proposed by the Critical Ancient World Studies project, discussed below—or different ways of engaging with those worlds altogether. Because despite Classics' hegemonic claim to knowing the Greek and Roman worlds, that knowledge exceeds it: it is created and circulates both within and without the academic discipline. Outside of education and research contexts, interest in these worlds is far from vulnerable—and always evolving. In the 21st-century United Kingdom, the

Greek and Roman worlds are flourishing, more accessible than ever for most people: theatre productions, novels, and films based on ancient myth and history proliferate; museums hold huge collections of Greek and Roman antiquities that are often free to visit; documentaries appear on broadcast television regularly, along with written works of popular history and myth. And beyond this, the actual 'stuff'—ideas, artefacts, stories, sites—of these ancient worlds are not generally in danger in the United Kingdom. Even while the academic discipline may decline, knowledge claimed by the discipline as 'the classical' continues to be produced and circulate between stakeholders in ever-evolving ways. Professional classicists may lament this, arguing (from a variety of political perspectives) that the academic discipline and its practitioners 'know best', but central to the discussions contained in this volume is the contention that the discipline knows that which it lays claim to only *in certain ways*: the discipline is *not* the knowledge and there always have been, and will continue to be, other ways of knowing those worlds in the present.

Understanding the relationship between Classics and knowledge of the Greek and Roman worlds—including the ways and effects of collapsing the two and assuming the discipline-as-knowledge—requires a look at the stakeholders of all kinds that make up the discipline and that also trade in interests in the ancient Greek and Roman worlds, as well as the interrelations between these stakeholders. The language of evolution and extinction suggests a way of conceptualising these stakeholders and interrelations: as an ecology. As Gregory Bateson writes in *Steps to an Ecology of Mind* (1972), 'ecology, in the widest sense, turns out to be the study of the interaction and survival of ideas and programs (i.e. differences, complexes of differences, etc.) in circuits'. Bateson is discussing a 20th-century shift in thought about the 'unit of evolutionary survival' from taxa—'individual, family line, species, subspecies, etc.'—to ecosystems and related concepts (49). A like shift seems necessary in pursuit of a framework for study that moves away from traditional models of inheritance and reception that underpin the discipline of Classics and its attempts to think about the relationship between the ancient and modern worlds (including its own relationship to its subject matter). Given the substantial problems with these models, we wish to explore the value in a movement away from linearity and towards the ecological.[4] This promises, we (the editors and authors of this volume) think, to be a generative way of reconceiving Classics and the worlds it is interested in.

Thinking Ecologically

In theatre studies, ecology has been used in recent years to approach, among other subjects, participation (Harpin and Nicholson), amateur theatre (Nicholson, Holdsworth, and Milling), precarity (Fragkou), and theatre and performance themselves (Kershaw), as well as, of course, the environment.[5]

This is part of a broader trend that has seen the term (mis)used beyond the scientific to mean, as per Jess Allen and Bronwyn Preece, 'a diversity and an interconnected complexity of ... [anything]' (91). While we are in danger of further misusing the term—not least by reading a system that produces and upholds inequality and imbalances of power through a metaphor that frames it as natural—there is much to be gained from positioning Classics and the knowledge it is concerned with in such a formulation. To begin with, identifying Classics as a multifarious network of constituents invested in, but separate from, the knowledge it claims—rather than synonymous with that knowledge—helps to *de*-naturalise systems, institutions, and claims that seek to appear natural. At the same time, the notion of ecology emphasises the flows and exchanges of knowledge between constituents, both in and outside of Classics, clarifying that the knowledge cannot rightly be said to be owned by certain individuals or organisations. It also understands the production and transfer of that knowledge as dependent on a complex set of interrelations impacted by individual idiosyncrasies and wider social, cultural, and political factors. This is a helpful counter to pervasive existing ideas that something special about the Greek and Roman worlds has allowed knowledge of them to survive to the present.

Ecology offers a shift in thinking away from assumptions of linearity that abet the notion of Greek and Roman—and thus Classics'—exceptionalism, the 'classical tradition' narrative predicated on Eurocentric progress and inheritance that excludes and orientalises those demarcated beyond the classical (e.g., the Muslim world).[6] The notion of ecology 'fundamentally emphasises the inseparable and reflexive interrelational and interdependent qualities of systems *as* systems' (Kershaw 16, emphasis original). It specialises in dealing with complexity and interrelationality—or, after Harpin and Nicholson, 'messiness' (5).[7] This explains why theatre scholars, among those from other fields, have turned to ecology to contend with the inherent messiness of their diffuse but nevertheless interconnected areas of interest; Kershaw remarks on how his reading on ecology resonated with his knowledge as a theatre maker that 'there are complicated and unavoidable interdependencies between every element of a performance event and its environment ... the smallest change to one factor of theatrical performance in some way, however minutely, will effect change in all the rest' (24). The question for Classics, therefore, is who or what makes up these interdependencies?

Traditionally, the constituent elements of the discipline of Classics might be limited to university scholars and their students. We, by contrast, propose that these are just one part of a wider, 'messy' system of relations, which we frame here as the Classics ecology. This resituates scholars from a privileged position of ownership over the knowledge of the ancient Greek and Roman worlds. Instead, they become one of many stakeholders that produce and regulate this knowledge: individuals with varying degrees of capital (in multiple senses), from school-age learners to academics to politicians, as well as organisations (schools, universities, museums, outreach charities, learned societies, publishers, broadcasters, etc.). These constituents attend to and transfer knowledge via practices and traditions (especially pedagogical) that take place in certain environments (natural, political, and otherwise). What distinguishes this particular ecology is its coherence around the (im)material 'stuff' of the ancient Greek and Roman worlds—texts, archaeological remains, myths, and so on. Crucially, however, an ecological approach understands this 'stuff' not as possessing and communicating its own self-evident meaning and value, but rather as subject to ever-shifting meaning and value as a result of the interrelations with and between individuals, organisations, and environments in the ecosystem. This is not to suggest that all constituents of the ecology are equally empowered to determine meaning and value: in fact, the imbalance of power is a central characteristic of the Classics ecology in particular, which replicates and affirms wider societal imbalances of power. This is most visible, perhaps, in long-running debates around elitism and social capital among those engaging with both the ancient Greek and Roman worlds and the academic discipline of Classics.[8]

Meanings and values change as the ecology and its constituents change. This has become apparent in the emergence of classical reception studies in the last few decades, which is perhaps one reason why the development of the sub-field has been (and, in some ways, continues to be) contentious. But some of the thinking around reception obscures how these meanings and values change. As Margherita Laera observes in her work on Greek tragedy, there is a tendency for classical reception to ascribe agency to the 'stuff' of the ancient Greek and Roman worlds in its 'abilities' or 'capacities' to 'survive' rather than focusing on the 'responsibility of the "receptor" in returning to those sources' (58). Perhaps conversely given the semantic associations of natural selection, the notion of a Classics ecology emphasises how its constituents actively *conserve* knowledge, rather than understanding that knowledge to have *survived* because of any kind of exceptional quality. That is to say, the constituent agents of the ecology have worked actively to preserve particular ways of knowing the ancient world to suit certain purposes, which have become dominant to the extent of being naturalised. This has often come at the expense of other ways of knowing global pasts.

In this sense, the Classics ecology operates as a 'multifaceted field of cultural production', in line with Nicholson, Holdsworth, and Milling's use of ecology (6). Consider the example of Sophocles' *Antigone*. A text exists, but one that has been edited, amended, and interpreted by successive generations of scholars. Understanding what the words of the text mean is not straightforward: translation of ancient Greek depends on traditions of interpretation. Greek-English lexicons that might be consulted are influenced by the ideologies of when, where, and by whom they were compiled.[9] Thus, translations from the Greek stand to be inflected by these layers of prior interpretation, and understanding based on a translated text (which is to say the understanding of the vast majority of people in the United Kingdom in the 21st century) is inflected in turn by both those prior interpretations and the particular character of the translation in question: Richard Jebb's 1891 translation has a different tone from Don Taylor's 1986 translation and again from those by Hugh Lloyd-Jones (1994), Timberlake Wertenbaker (1998), and Anne Carson (2015). We highlight these because they are publicly available via digital means.[10] As this indicates, many publicly available translations are at least 25 years old at the time of writing, and as many people are neither willing nor able to purchase expensive up-to-date academic books, they must rely on what is freely available. This impacts the flow of knowledge about *Antigone*.

Taylor's text was used by the BBC for their 1986 television adaptation and again by the National Theatre of Great Britain for their 2012 production, one of many productions of the play staged in the United Kingdom in the last two decades; recordings of both are available via digital platforms widely used by educational institutions to facilitate the teaching of *Antigone*. The play is a set text on A level syllabi in both Classics and drama-based subjects (the OCR Drama A level syllabus stipulates Jean Anouilh's 1942 version but also recommends a recording of the BBC version available on YouTube).[11] Not long after the National's production, Jatinder Verma of London-based Tara Theatre suggested novelist Kamila Shamsie adapt *Antigone* into a play; instead it became a novel, *Home Fire*, reimagining the story in the context of 21st-century British Muslim experience and British governmental hostility to Muslims.[12] Shamsie credits her understanding of *Antigone* to versions by Carson and by Seamus Heaney (2005), as well as Ali Smith's 2013 retelling for children (275). This points to the numerous other recent retellings and interpretations that exist outside of the context of *Antigone* as a play, in the writings of (among others) Judith Butler, Bonnie Honig, and Helen Morales. These examples are far from comprehensive, but they indicate that the reading, teaching, and staging of *Antigone* is shaped as much by the complex interrelations of modern humans and their ideas operating as part of wider organisations and networks as by the text attributed to Sophocles, with interest in that text sustained by those same organisations and networks. As a result, there is considerable variation in the meanings and values associated with *Antigone* despite the seemingly stable presence of its text (although such variation might be broken down into trends).

Part of the usefulness of ecology as a concept is to foreground a distinction between object and idea—for example, the text called *Antigone* and the many iterations and interpretations of it—and to dislodge assumptions about fixity of meaning and value, emphasising the notion of these changing through the ecology. As Mathura Umachandran and Marchella Ward make clear in the introduction to *Critical Ancient World Studies: The Case for Forgetting Classics*, the academic discipline called Classics is predicated on fixed meanings and values associated with the ancient Greek and Roman worlds that are very often elevated to the universal. This is the first principle of Umachandran and Ward's manifesto for Critical Ancient World Studies (CAWS):

> [CAWS] critiques the field's Eurocentrism and refuses to inherit silently a field crafted so as to constitute a mythical pre-history for an imagined 'West', in particular, by rejecting the 'universal' as synonym for the 'Western' or the 'European'. While Classics has been content to construct an ancient world whose value lies in its mirror image of modern Europe, CAWS investigates the ancient history of a world without accepting the *telos* of the West. (3)

We see our project as cognate with the aims of CAWS because the notion of an ecology situates this *telos*, this idea of a mythical pre-history, the very concept of a 'classical tradition' or 'inheritance' that connects the 'West' to ancient Greece and Rome in a golden genealogical line of descent, as in fact produced and sustained by the interrelations that make up the ecology. The shift from genealogy to ecology might still understand the later influence of these ancient cultures in terms of tradition, but in doing so it emphasises the role of those constituents of the ecology in producing, maintaining, and transmitting that tradition—fabricating it, investing in it, believing in it—rather than as accepting the tradition in terms easily colluded into troubling worldviews.

The dominating role of the academic discipline of Classics in this ecology skews the latter's character so that it is both conservative and conservational. The debate around Classics' extinction or evolution turns out to be a manifestation of this. Because the ecology conserves knowledge of the ancient Greek and Roman worlds in a manner that is often motivated by a belief in those worlds' universal value, articulations of threat and the need for survival help in that conservation by establishing a persistent sense of impending, catastrophic loss *unless action is taken*—in other words, unless constituents of the ecology help to stimulate it further. The call to action and the sense of catastrophe are reciprocal, each reinforcing the belief in the exceptionality of both the ancient Greek and Roman worlds and the academic discipline of Classics. As the discipline positions itself as functionally identical to the knowledge it conserves—presenting, essentially, the discipline-as-knowledge—it assumes exceptional status at the same time as it comes under threat and in need of saving for its own sake. Participating in or upholding the discipline of Classics is therefore construed as appropriate conservational action to preserve the threatened and universally valuable knowledge of ancient Greece and Rome. It is for this reason that we talk about a 'Classics ecology', rather than, for example, an 'ancient world ecology': the discipline is hegemonic within these systems. But nevertheless Classics remains only one part of the ecology, and, as we have established, it is not the same as the knowledge it claims; while the collapse of Classics in the United Kingdom (or elsewhere) would indeed be a loss—not least in terms of employment—it would be the discipline but not the associated knowledge that goes 'extinct', because that knowledge flows through other parts of the ecology. The ecology would be impacted, certainly, but the knowledge would flow in different ways.

An illustrative example of this conservative and conservational character can be found in the work of Natalie Haynes, one of the leading public figures associated with the ancient Greek and Roman worlds in the United Kingdom today. After studying Classics at Cambridge, Haynes began a career as a stand-up comedian, broadcaster, and author. Since 2014, she has had a BBC Radio 4 show, *Natalie Haynes Stands Up for the Classics*, which in punning on her light-hearted approach and her status as promoter of ancient Greek and Roman worlds demonstrates the collapse of discipline and knowledge and the conservational impulse. It is also since 2014 that Haynes has published a successful series of books that rewrite ancient Greek myth from different perspectives than those commonly found in ancient sources, such as the Trojan War-based *A Thousand Ships* (2019), which 'gives voices to the women, girls and goddesses who, for so long, have been silent' ('A Thousand Ships'). In this way, Haynes appears to critique ancient texts and their authors in ways that are akin to the feminist practice of 're-visioning' (Rich). But taken alongside Haynes' other public written and spoken comments that perpetuate the notion of ancient Greece and Rome as superlative and universal, her books seem instead to reinscribe the essential value of the ancient sources with which she appears to contend.[13] This seeming paradox—that ancient texts can be universal, greater than all others, and yet complicit in silencing certain voices and so in need of modern contention—speaks to the way the Classics ecology circulates ideas about the ancient Greek and Roman worlds that are conserved by a validating notion of tradition while also being (re)produced through changing interrelations within the ecology.

Haynes' approach is antithetical to the one exemplified by Boris Johnson, whose well-known affection for the cultures of Greece and Rome directly supports his conservativism.[14] Haynes envisions Classics as progressive: fun, relevant, harmonious with modern popular culture, and a great social equaliser. In 2016, Haynes resigned as a patron for Classics for All, which promotes the teaching of Classics in UK schools, over the charity's continued association with Johnson. Haynes described Johnson as a 'dog-whistling racist and misogynist' for comments made about Muslim women, explaining that she could not 'defend [Classics for All] if it chooses to stand behind a man whose every utterance conveys that only some people are worth being included under the banner of "all"'. The charity responded by affirming that they 'do not endorse or support Boris Johnson's statement or comments' (Di Steffano). Despite this clash of sensibilities, both Haynes and Johnson had previously co-existed in the project of a Classics that is universally applicable. Where a progressive vision employs the rhetoric of universality and genealogy, as Haynes and similar advocates such as Stephen Fry frequently do, it reveals itself as entangled with the conservative vision. As Umachandran and Ward argue, 'many of the assumptions that permit and legitimate such uses of the ancient world in support of white supremacist, ableist, Islamophobic or otherwise hateful aims are not only evident in mis-uses of the ancient world, but are fundamental to the structures of knowledge formation in the discipline known as "Classics"' (4). Haynes and Classics for All may not endorse Johnson's Islamophobia but, as Ward demonstrates, uncritically embracing '"the classical" as a pseudo-temporal category' results in disciplinary Islamophobia ('Remaking Temporality').[15] The constitution of the discipline of Classics thus skews the ecology it dominates towards the conservative. Figures such as Haynes may strive, for good reasons and with good intentions, to relocate knowledge of the ancient Greek and Roman worlds so that right wing, exclusionary uses are aberrations, but they are, in fact, embedded into the ecology.

In Haynes' address at the 2023 Classical Association conference, she reaffirmed the notion of Classics for all in the sense that the knowledge conserved by the discipline empowers individuals to do anything they want. This is a line of thought that responds to recent rhetoric against the humanities more broadly and demonstrates how the concept of threat can be turned to conservative/conservational ends. It resonates with Umachandran and Ward's discussion of similar comments in Helen Morales' *Antigone Rising* (2020), a book that makes use of the ecologically conceived modern understanding of *Antigone* as the foundation for a progressive politics. In spite of these aspirations, Umachandran and Ward identify a conservatism to this rhetoric:

> 'Who owns antiquity? Who owns culture?'—Helen Morales answers triumphantly, 'We do'. Morales' question, despite its optimistic aspirations to inclusion, serves to reinscribe a model of ownership in the study of classical antiquity ... Morales' question also pre-supposes a universal 'we', a category made up of unmarked bodies that function as natural inheritors of this ancient past—and who do not struggle to access the room of the universal. ... The idea of a universal 'we' in the study of antiquity is its own particular kind of violence, that erases the various ways that antiquity is kept from certain groups and shared out freely to others. (13)

In thinking through Haynes' work ecologically, it becomes clear that—despite similar 'optimistic aspirations to inclusion'—such work overlooks the networks of privilege that do continue to structure the circulation and use of knowledge of ancient Greek and Roman worlds; it is these networks that helped bring people like Johnson to prominence. Two particularly privileged (and interrelated) networks that facilitate much cultural power in the United Kingdom are those of the Universities of Oxford and Cambridge. In both 2010 and 2017, Labour MP David Lammy's freedom of information requests to the universities showed that their students continued to be overwhelmingly white, from the south of England, and from 'the top two social classes' (Lammy).[16] Many of the most influential constituents in the Classics ecology studied at Oxbridge. Of the 20 recipients of the Classical Association Prize, 'awarded annually to the person, group, or project whose work is felt to have raised the profile of Classics in the public eye' ('The CA Prize'), over half are graduates of Oxbridge, and three quarters received the prize for work associated with or promoted by Oxbridge. The landscape of Classics in UK higher education is significantly shaped by Oxbridge: research published in 2017 showed that an overwhelming 84% of academics in the 20 largest Classics departments in the United Kingdom had studied at Oxford or Cambridge either as undergraduates or postgraduates (Richardson; compared to 66% in English departments). These individuals may not all be from the privileged areas Lammy identified—and the elite status of an Oxbridge education does not automatically equate to the promulgation of elitism—but it is hardly a surprise that a damning 2024 report found that professional classicists are among the ten most elitist professions in the United Kingdom (Canevaro et al). It seems that not only are egalitarian visions of Classics inescapably bound up with the elite (and elitist) power dynamics that run through the Classics ecology but that the ecology rewards participation in a certain definition of Classics.

Tragedy, Education, and Theatre Practices in the UK Classics Ecology

In this volume, as a first foray into the Classics ecology, we have narrowed our scope to the ecological interrelations among Greek tragedy, theatre practices, and education. Our exploration concerns a Classics ecology based in the United Kingdom, and although there are of course other national ecologies and indeed a global ecology, we seek here to think about the multitude of complexities in the United Kingdom alone, not least due to the United Kingdom's colonial context of Classics. As such, our concern is also with theatre and education in the United Kingdom. There is a long and distinctive history of Classics in the United Kingdom (and its interrelations with theatre and education), as has been well documented elsewhere,[17] and we maintain that the 'shape' of this history is not a line but an ecological system. Our focus here is on that system primarily in the last two decades, though many of the chapters necessarily look back further. Likewise, we focus on Greek tragedy because it has a rich, ongoing presence in the ecology in this period. In terms of education, the chapters skew towards higher education and the related work of scholarship, though there are references to other forms of education; we acknowledge, even so, that this focus excludes a more varied ecology, in part because of the ableism and other exclusionary practices of UK higher education. However, when it comes to theatre, our focus is on a polymorphous range of practices: the chapters variously discuss British theatre as found in high-profile venues such as the National Theatre, as well as fringe theatre companies, universities, drama schools, and multiple small, idiosyncratic projects that themselves are fascinating ecological products.

These limitations noted, why this focus? Simply put, it makes an excellent test case for thinking ecologically, for multiple reasons. As indicated by the discussion of *Antigone* above, Greek tragedy is a prime example of what we mean when we say that the knowledge conserved by the Classics ecology deals in shifting ideas rather than fixed objects, though the ideas bear relation to objects. The term 'Greek tragedy' itself indicates an idea more than a set of objects. Although it notionally refers to texts and/or performance practices that emerged exclusively in Athens in a relatively brief part of the city's history before spreading elsewhere in the ancient world, the generic label 'Greek' flattens out the permutations of historical change so that other ideas, notably Aristotle's belated analysis in *Poetics*, get included: multiple A level syllabi in the United Kingdom require students to learn about *Poetics* in the same unit as they study the texts of Aeschylus, Sophocles, and Euripides.[18] The word 'tragedy', too, brings in misleading genealogies, making ancient Athenian playwrights appear to have been working on the same kind of theatre as later authors, such as Shakespeare, allowing anachronistic expectations to creep in that rarely account for the ideological motivations of (early) modern Europeans and others seeking to position themselves as part of the 'West' 'returning' to 'the Greeks'. Greek tragedy, therefore, is an example of an idea produced and maintained in the Classics ecology.

It is in seeking to better understand how the idea of Greek tragedy circulates that we have decided to focus on theatre and education. As Kershaw theorised, theatre itself can be understood as an ecology, and so might education in the United Kingdom today. Part of Kershaw's analysis draws on what ecologists call 'edge effects', phenomena that occur in an 'ecotone'—that is, a place where 'two or more distinctive ecologies rub up against each other' (185). Thus, we see the rubbing up of UK Classics with theatre and educational ecologies as a potentially productive 'ecotone' for analysis; in this formulation, the idea of Greek tragedy might be conceived of as itself an edge effect, or perhaps rather an idea construed through multiple differing edge effects. As the chapters collectively make clear, both ecology and ecotone are dependent on, and influenced by, institutions, practices, and knowledge(s) beyond those that are centred in Classics as a discipline. Moreover, the edge effects produced in this collision of three ecologies do not exclusively concern or return to Greek tragedy, a productive decentring that is a helpful reminder of the fact that, however, much Classics and Greek tragedy might be valued by some (including by the editors and authors in this volume), they are part of something much wider in the 21st-century United Kingdom.

The contributions in this volume have been written by both theatre makers and academics; their backgrounds vary between theatre studies and Classics. Some make use of the notion of ecology explicitly, while others address it implicitly in their attentiveness to networks, knowledge flows, and so on; the outcomes of these uses vary. In addition, the chapters present a wide range of methodologies and approaches and although we have undertaken to make these as intelligible as possible across disciplinary and practical boundaries, we have not enforced an artificial consensus. As such, the chapters themselves might produce their own equivalents of edge effects as they rub up alongside one another in this volume-as-ecotone.

The chapters in Part I, 'Mediating Knowledge(s)', explore how forms of knowledge are accessed, employed, processed, and transmitted in projects that engage with Greek tragedy. Christine Plastow's chapter begins from a particularly visible meeting point between Classics academia and Greek tragedy, the academic consultant in professional theatre practice. It examines a selection of ways in which classicists can work with theatre makers, identifying models for interactions between Classics academics and theatre practitioners and exploring how each makes use of different types of knowledge. Then, David Bullen considers the creation, flow, and transformation of knowledge in two organisations poised between theatre and Classics, the University of Oxford's Archive of Performances of Greek and Roman Drama and theatre company Actors of Dionysus. Finally, Peter Swallow brings this discussion more fully into a higher education context by exploring the long history of King's College London's annual production of an ancient Greek play through its relations to the various stakeholders and goals of the Classics department. Using extensive archival research, Swallow shows how developments in the play over its lifetime have interacted with and responded to other constituents in the Classics ecology to emphasise particular knowledges.

Part II, 'Choral Practice and Participation', explores theories and practices of theatre making through the chorus. Stephe Harrop sets out ways in which actors in training learn through activities based on the chorus, particularly those derived from the influential approaches of Jacques Lecoq. Harrop shows how such activities often reduce the chorus to a symbol of unity and cohesion, which plays a part in problematic perceptions of Greek drama that elide contest and debate. Chapters 6 and 7 then offer contrasting portraits of the value of choral participation. Practitioners Helen Eastman and Alex Silverman reflect on a series of choral projects they have led in the United Kingdom and abroad, unpacking how these offer pedagogical opportunities beyond learning about Greek theatre that support understanding of (for example) theatrical skills, group identity, consensus and compromise. They reflect on connections to the originary role of Greek choruses and identify instances where choral practice reveals disagreement and can present challenges. Sarah Weston, meanwhile, employs interviews with participants in community chorus projects to reflect on the value of such projects for both participants and theatre makers; she explores community as a concept and considers how ideals for the community chorus meet actual practices, particularly rehearsal processes, expectations of professionalism and (lack of) pay. Her analysis reveals that while many participants have positive experiences in community choruses, idealising associations of Greek tragedy with democracy (as also outlined by Harrop) can often mask challenges in this type of work and even exploitative practices.

The final part, 'Academics and/as Practitioners', offers two case studies that revisit a theme that runs throughout the volume: practical relationships between scholars and theatre makers and what this makes visible about how knowledge is valued and shared. Lottie Parkyn reflects on Sheffest, a festival celebrating ancient Greek drama she co-organised in 2012. Of all the volume's contributors, Parkyn employs the concept of the Classics ecology most explicitly, drawing attention to assumptions of inherent value attached to ancient Greek culture that the ecology maintains. Parkyn questions 'outreach' that emerges from the ecology, framing the discussion in relation to debates about democratising culture—attempts to widen access to a predetermined understanding of cultural value—versus cultural democracy, whereby communities define culture on their terms. Then, in the final chapter, Laura Swift reflects on her experience in co-producing the play *Fragments* with artists from Potential Difference. Swift explores the unique potential of fragmentary tragedies for collaborative work between theatre makers and academics, reflecting on the varied approaches the team took to the source material, including methods derived from psychology. She notes how ancient fragments are not only interesting as texts for performance, but also create space for interpretation that may be scholarly or creative, and in this way expand access to the ancient world.

In setting out our framework of the Classics ecology, we hope to present a provocation: that it is worthwhile to consider not only the 'stuff' of Classics, and not only the history of the discipline of Classics, but the operation of Classics as a discipline in and out of the academy and in particular the impact this operation has on knowledge(s), and on access to, and circulation of, knowledge(s). By engaging with the ancient world, we all become constituents in the ecology; by becoming aware of the ecology, we can assess how far our actions within it go to perpetuate or disrupt existing knowledge structures. The ecology allows us to perceive with equal significance the contributions of scholars, creative practitioners, broadcasters, and curators, as well as politicians, students at all levels, amateur historians, and many others to understanding of what 'Classics' is. By understanding what it is (and is not), it is possible to think about what it might be. While this volume necessarily narrows its focus, we hope that the Classics ecology might prove a useful lens to explore other topics. For now, we offer our exploration of Greek tragedy as a case study—we, at least, plan to go from there.

Notes

1 For a brief outline and further details, see 'Oxford and Colonialism'.
2 Morley makes a similar case.

3 See, for example, Higgins. For a fuller discussion of the closures Higgins was objecting to, see Bullen.
4 For the problems, see Umachandran and Ward.
5 See Woynarski 7–19; Kershaw 26–30.
6 See Ward, 'Remaking Temporality': 'the linear timeline of the classical has allowed Classics to function as a kind of European futurism, using the ancient past to legitimate Europe's supremacy' (181).
7 Other scholars have engaged with theoretical 'messiness' in critiquing the discipline of Classics; see e.g. Hamilakis and Jones, Khellaf, and Ward, 'Remaking Temporality'.
8 See Hunt and Holmes-Henderson for disparities at school level; see Hall and Stead for historical engagements with Classics across class boundaries in the United Kingdom.
9 Liddell and Scott's 1889 lexicon, the standard in the field, was only updated in 2021; see Flood for coverage of the Victorianisms this brought to light.
10 Jebb's is the English translation on the free *Perseus Digital Library* and Lloyd-Jones's is in the digital Loeb Classical Library, while Taylor's, Wertenbaker's, and Carson's are provided on Drama Online, a digital library widely used in UK drama teaching.
11 AQA's Drama A level syllabus stipulates Robert Fagles' 1984 translation, as does the Cambridge Assessment International Education's Classical Studies A level syllabus. The APGRD database shows that *Antigone* is the second most performed Greek tragedy in 21st-century British theatre, after Euripides' *Medea*.
12 *Antigone* has also provided a format for other playwrights to explore Islamophobia in modern Britain: see Ward, 'An ancient play of the moment'; 'Inua Ellams in Conversation with Helen Eastman.'
13 In 2018, for example, when the *Odyssey* topped a methodologically dubious attempt by BBC Culture to rank the top hundred stories that 'shaped the world', Haynes wrote an article asking rhetorically whether the *Odyssey* is 'the greatest tale ever told?' (Haynes).
14 For example, Johnson's *The Dream of Rome* employed his interpretation of Rome's success to support his arguments for leaving the European Union.
15 Umachandran and Ward do not discuss the Haynes/Johnson incident but do single out Classics for All's 'impassioned vaunting of the western civilisation narrative' (5).
16 It is worth noting that Oxbridge's privileging of elite students from the south of England maps onto the findings of Hunt and Holmes-Henderson—it is state-maintained schools outside of the south of England that experience 'A level Classics poverty'.
17 See, for example, Hall and Macintosh; Hall and Stead.
18 On the distorting legacy of Aristotle on the study and practice of Greek tragedy, see Dunbar and Harrop (27–51).

Works Cited

Allen, Jess, and Bronwyn Preece. 'Decentring the Stage: Towards an Ecocentric Ethics of Performance.' *Performing Ethos: International Journal of Ethics in Theatre & Performance* 5.1 (2015): 3–15.

APGRD YouTube Channel. 'Inua Ellams in Conversation with Helen Eastman.' *APGRD YouTube Channel*, 31 Oct. 2022, www.youtube.com/watch?app=desktop&v=tXFiXyDE8UY. Accessed 1 Aug. 2023.

Bateson, Gregory. *Steps to an Ecology of Mind*. University of Chicago Press, 1972/2000.

Bullen, David. 'Saving Classics with the *Clouds*: A Case Study in Adapting Aristophanes.' *Aristophanic Humour: Theory and Practice*, edited by Peter Swallow and Edith Hall, Bloomsbury, 2020, 205–214.

Butterfield, David. 'Classics in UK Universities: Cui Bono?' *Antigone*, 2022, www.antigonejournal.com/2022/05/classics-uk-universities. Accessed 1 Aug. 2023.

Canevaro, Lilah Grace, Mirko Canevaro, Bianca Mazzinghi Gori, Henry Stead, and Eris B. Williams Reed. *Class in Classics*. University of Edinburgh, 2024.

Carson, Anne, translator. *Antigone*. By Sophocles. Oberon, 2015.

'Decline & Fall: Classics Edition: On Identity Politics in Classical Studies.' *New Criterion*, Mar. 2019, www.newcriterion.com/issues/2019/3/decline-fall-classics-edition. Accessed 1 Aug. 2023.

Di Steffano, Mark. 'Two Female Authors Said They'll Resign from a Charity Where Boris Johnson Is a Patron.' *Buzzfeed*, 17 Aug. 2018, www.buzzfeed.com/markdistefano/this-bbc-broadcaster-penned-a-scorching-letter-of. Accessed 1 Aug. 2023.

Dunbar, Zachary, and Stephe Harrop. *Greek Tragedy and the Contemporary Actor*. Palgrave Macmillan, 2018.

Flood, Alison. 'English Dictionary of Ancient Greek "Spares No Blushes" with Fresh Look at Crudity.' *The Guardian*, 27 May 2021, www.theguardian.com/books/2021/may/27/first-english-dictionary-of-ancient-greek-since-victorian-era-spares-no-blushes-lexicon-classics. Accessed 7 Aug. 2023.

Fragkou, Marissa. *Ecologies of Precarity in Twenty-First Century Theatre: Politics, Affect, Responsibility*. Bloomsbury, 2019.

Hall, Edith, and Fiona Macintosh. *Greek Tragedy and the British Theatre 1660–1914*. Oxford University Press, 2005.

Hall, Edith, and Henry Stead. *A People's History of Classics: Class and Greco-Roman Antiquity in Britain and Ireland 1689 to 1939*. Routledge, 2020.

Hamilakis, Yannis, and Andrew Meirion Jones. 'Archaeology and Assemblage.' *Cambridge Archaeological Journal* 27.1 (2017): 77–84.

Harpin, Anna, and Helen Nicholson. 'Performance and Participation.' *Performance and Participation: Practices, Audiences, Politics*, edited by Anna Harpin and Helen Nicholson, Palgrave, 2017, 1–15.

Haynes, Natalie. *A Thousand Ships*. *Natalie Haynes*, https://nataliehaynes.com/books/a-thousand-ships. Accessed 1 Aug. 2023.

Haynes, Natalie. 'The Greatest Tale Ever Told?' *BBC Culture*, 22 May 2018, www.bbc.com/culture/article/20180521-the-greatest-tale-ever-told. Accessed 8 Aug. 2023.

Heaney, Seamus. *The Burial at Thebes: Sophocles' Antigone*. Faber and Faber, 2005.

Higgins, Charlotte. 'Classics at risk at Royal Holloway, University of London.' *The Guardian*, 15 Sep. 2011, www.theguardian.com/culture/charlottehigginsblog/2011/sep/15/educationdegreecourses-classics. Accessed 1 Aug. 2023.

Hunt, Steven, and Arlene Holmes-Henderson. 'A Level Classics Poverty: Classical Subjects in Schools in England: Access, Attainment and Progression.' *Council of University Classical Departments Bulletin* 50 (2021): 1–26.

Johnson, Boris. *The Dream of Rome*. HarperCollins, 2006.

Kershaw, Baz. *Theatre Ecology: Environments and Performance Events*. Cambridge University Press, 2007.

Khellaf, Kyle. 'Classical Nomadologies.' *Ramus* 49 (2020): 1–40.

Laera, Margherita. *Reaching Athens: Community, Democracy, and Other Mythologies in Adaptations of Greek Tragedy*. Peter Lang, 2013.

Lammy, David. 'Seven Years Have Changed Nothing at Oxbridge. In Fact, Diversity Is Even Worse.' *The Guardian*, 20 Oct. 2017, www.theguardian.com/commentisfree/2017/oct/20/oxford-cambridge-not-changed-diversity-even-worse-admissions. Accessed 8 Aug. 2023.

Lloyd-Jones, Hugh, editor and translator. *Sophocles: Antigone, Women of Trachis, Philoctetes, Oedipus at Colonus*. Harvard University Press, 1994.

Marshall, Sharon. 'Classics at UK Universities, 2019–20: Statistics.' *Council of University Classical Departments Bulletin* 50 (2021), https//cucd.blogs.sas.ac.uk/files/2021/09/CUCD-stats-2020.pdf. Accessed 1 Aug. 2023.

Morales, Helen. *Antigone Rising: The Subversive Power of the Ancient Myths*. Bold Type Books, 2020.

Morley, Neville. *Classics: Why It Matters*. Polity, 2018.

Nicholson, Helen, Nadine Holdsworth, and Jane Milling. *The Ecologies of Amateur Theatre*. Palgrave Macmillan, 2018.

'Oxford and Colonialism: Faculty of Classics.' *Oxford and Colonialism*, https//oxfordandcolonialism.web.ox.ac.uk/faculty-of-classics. Accessed 8 Aug. 2023.

Poser, Rachel. 'He Wants to Save Classics from Whiteness. Can the Field Survive?' *New York Times Magazine*, 2 Feb. 2021, www.nytimes.com/2021/02/02/magazine/classics-greece-rome-whiteness.html. Accessed 1 Aug. 2023.

Rich, Adrienne. *On Lies, Secrets, and Silence: Selected Prose 1966–1978*. Norton, 1979.

Shamsie, Kamila. *Home Fire*. Bloomsbury, 2017.

'The CA Prize.' *The Classical Association*, www.classicalassociation.org/the-classical-association-prize. Accessed 1 Aug. 2023.

Umachandran, Mathura, and Marchella Ward. 'Towards a Manifesto for Critical Ancient World Studies.' *Critical Ancient World Studies: The Case for Forgetting Classics*, edited by Mathura Umachandran and Marchella Ward, Routledge, 2023, 3–34.

Ward, Marchella. 'An Ancient Play of the Moment: What Antigone Could Mean for the Modern World.' *TLS*, 29 Oct. 2021, www.the-tls.co.uk/articles/what-antigone-could-mean-for-the-modern-world-essay-marchella-ward. Accessed 1 Aug. 2023.

———. 'Queer Time, Crip Time, Woman Time, Sick Time, Sleepy Time, Muslim Time… Remaking Temporality Beyond "the Classical".' *Critical Ancient World Studies: The Case for Forgetting Classics*, edited by Mathura Umachandran and Marchella Ward, Routledge, 2023, 172–188.

Wertenbaker, Timberlake. *Oedipus Plays: Oedipus Tyrannos, Oedipus at Kolonos, Antigone*. Faber and Faber, 1998.

Woynarski, Lisa. *Ecodramaturgies: Theatre, Performance and Climate Change*. Palgrave Macmillan, 2020.

Part I
Mediating Knowledge(s)

2 Towards Co-creation

Roles of Classics Academics in Modern Productions of Greek Tragedy

Christine Plastow

Introduction

The involvement of Classics academics in theatrical productions based on Greek tragedy is nothing new. For years, some of the greatest interest in staging tragedies came from inside universities, where productions were put on in the original Greek. The emphasis of these productions was squarely on the value of the tragedies as classical texts, with little attention paid to theatricality, at least in a professional sense. But as Greek tragedy moved out of universities, and out of Greek, into productions in English on the professional British stage, academic input came with them. This is, partially, a symptom of the form: Greek tragedies were written in an ancient language not widely accessible to those without an (historically elite) education, and thus have usually required, at minimum, the involvement of a competent translator. As a range of accurate translations for the most commonly staged tragedies have become more readily available over the years, and as playwrights without knowledge of the ancient language have developed their own new versions through access to these translations, the (obvious) involvement of academics in this part of the process has decreased; nevertheless, professional classicists have retained a role in the making of (especially high-profile) productions of Greek tragedy on the British stage.[1] Perhaps this is because, despite the increased presence and popularity of Greek tragedy in the modern theatre, its origins remain somewhat distant and, at times, strange and obscure: the context and conventions of the ancient theatre were utterly different from those of modern British theatre, as was the society in which it was produced. Despite efforts to broaden access to classical subjects in education, expertise in the topic remains the preserve of academics, particularly those associated with a few top universities.

In this chapter, I explore some of the ways in which Classics academia has been involved in modern productions of Greek tragedy, primarily through the involvement of individual academics in the production process. Academic involvement in theatrical production has taken a range of forms, and three will be explored here: the academic translator, the consultant, and

DOI: 10.4324/b22844-3

the co-creator. I am interested in the ways these projects construct, prioritise, and combine different kinds of knowledge. I do not aim to give an exhaustive overview of every instance of interaction between academics and theatre makers that has occurred in the United Kingdom: indeed, I necessarily cherry-pick examples of academics who have written about their experiences working on theatrical productions. Nor do I hope to capture the nuances of every possible working dynamic. Rather, I hope to outline some perceived models, consider their implications for the creation and circulation of knowledge within the Classics ecology, and propose some benefits of models that aim at co-creation rather than consultation.

The Academic Translator: Gilbert Murray

Greek tragedy has long held a place on the British stage, though often in heavily adapted forms (Hall and Macintosh). In the early 20th century, though, the first professional productions of Greek tragedy in English were staged at the Court Theatre by Harley Granville Barker (Hall 38). From these very first productions, there was academic involvement. The translations used by Barker were written by Gilbert Murray, a respected classicist; his academic career was interrupted by a period of ill health, during which he began to produce verse translations of both Greek comedy and tragedy. Though Murray's translations were criticised by contemporaries, most prominently by T. S. Eliot, as 'sub-Swinburnian obstructions which prevented the reader from accessing the Euripidean text' (Macintosh, 'From the Court' 148), it is clearer from the modern perspective that Murray's work combined suitably close attention to the Greek with a poetic flair that made the plays appealing to theatre makers like Barker as well as audiences; as Morwood puts it, he 'brought Greek tragedy to the professional 20th-century stage with an altogether unprecedented textual authenticity' (135).[2] His involvement with the stage production of his translations did not end with provision of the text, and Murray had productive relationships with Barker and with George Bernard Shaw both of whom actively looked to the translator for guidance in interpreting the plays. As David Bullen notes, Murray was 'an expert mediator between the ancient and modern worlds' ('Dionysus the New Woman' 53). When Barker's wife Lillah McCarthy spearheaded a production of Murray's translation of *Bacchae*, Murray's sway was such that he was able to veto the performance over his differences with the rather experimental director, William Poel, who viewed the play as 'purely satire' and would not account for Murray's belief in the 'profound connection between Greek tragedy and ritual practice' (57). Murray clearly felt that not only his text but his interpretation of the text should be considered important by the director; the classicist's view was, in his mind, essential to the successful staging of Greek tragedy. Despite the unusual nature of this case, it offers a useful background for considering what the role of the academic in theatre making has, can, and should be in the late 20th and 21st centuries.

The Academic Consultant: A Traditional Model

In the later part of the 20th century, the role of the academic translator in producing Greek tragedy on the modern stage diminished. Academic translations of ancient drama began to proliferate which were much more squarely focused on accuracy in representing the meaning of the ancient text than on performability. These translations facilitated the production by more performance-minded playwrights who did not read Greek of new adaptations and versions of Greek tragedy, which were better suited to the stage than translations designed for the classroom. Even playwrights who did read Greek and produced texts that could more clearly be called 'translations', such as the acclaimed author of classically inspired poetry and plays Tony Harrison, tended to be writers in the first instance, rather than academics turning their hand to writing play texts. Classical academic expertise, then, would begin to enter the rehearsal room in a different way: the role of the 'consultant'.

The two Classics academic consultants *par excellence* in Britain in the late 20th and 21st centuries have been Oliver Taplin and Edith Hall. Both are respected and widely published scholars in the field of Greek drama and have worked as consultants on several high-profile productions. Hall's influence has been widespread, consulting on many productions including the Old Vic's *Electra* in 2014, the RSC's *Hecuba* in 2015, and the Actors' Touring Company's *Suppliants* in 2017 ('Theatre by Edith Hall'). Besides two iterations of the *Oresteia* at the National Theatre which I will discuss below, Taplin has been involved in the Royal Shakespeare Company's 1991–92 production *The Thebans* and Tara Theatre's *Oedipus the King* in 1991, for example, as well as numerous overseas productions.[3] Taplin has written most extensively about his experiences, and so shall be my primary focus here.

Taplin had a somewhat informal presence in the rehearsal room for the development of Peter Hall's *Oresteia* at the National Theatre in 1981–82 and acted more formally as academic consultant for Katie Mitchell's production of the same trilogy in 1999–2000. Hall's production used a translation by Tony Harrison, and it was through Harrison that Taplin became involved in the production: Harrison had consulted Taplin's *The Stagecraft of Aeschylus* during his lengthy development of the script (Taplin, 'An academic' 12).[4] The translation was commissioned by Hall, and Hall and Harrison worked closely together on the script in order to realise Hall's vision, which had begun with his interest in masks (Parker 338); Taplin's book seems to have shaped Hall's choices in significant ways (Parker 343–345). Taplin wrote to Harrison and was invited to attend rehearsals (Taplin, 'An academic' 12). Here, both Harrison and Taplin had academic input on the production's development:

> My contribution, in so far as I had one, was through [Harrison]. We had many energetic conversations about the recurrent leitmotifs, the mirror-scenes, the significance of props and so on: for me it was an elating experience to find my

academic interests and research feeding into theatrical practice. We also had many conversations about details in the Greek—I remember the cast teasing their poet, 'off for your Greek lessons!'—and this led occasionally to changes as well as interpretations. (13)

In a later interview, Taplin characterised his work as an academic consultant on theatrical productions as follows:

> To a large extent I've found that my most productive input has been talking with the Director before rehearsals begin, or during the course of rehearsals ... I think actually my input in rehearsal, apart from being asked how on earth do you say this name, and that kind of thing, I couldn't say it's been that big. I've had more role in talking with the Director and what I've usually been able to do, in a terrifically unpredictable way, is the director talks about their interpretation or asks questions and I, more or less, pour out ideas and some of them they pick up and some of them they don't.
> (Hardwick)

It is clear, then, that for Taplin the value of the role of the consultant is in speaking with individuals in the creative team, in these instances the translator-playwright and the director, rather than being embedded in the team more widely. Taplin's emphasis on a minimal role in rehearsal also seems to chime with Jonathan Croall's account of the rehearsals of Peter Hall's *Bacchai* at the National Theatre in 2002: Edith Hall was present as an academic expert, but her interjections in this setting appear minimal in Croall's telling (20). Taplin characterises his work with the director as 'advising', 'talking with', and answering questions. The sense is of the academic consultant providing a source of knowledge which the creative practitioner(s) can use or not, as they see fit. Discussion often focuses on providing background information about ancient theatrical contexts and conventions, as well as 'poetic themes': for example, Taplin notes his discussions with Katie Mitchell about 'image clusters, networks of metaphor' around clothing in the *Oresteia* (Hardwick). He is keen to emphasise a distance between himself and the actual creative process: 'by talking in my quite professorial way about the clothing detail of *The Oresteia*, that did turn into something—but through the creativity of the director. I mean I couldn't claim for a moment that was my idea. I simply supplied some kind of catalyst for the idea' (Hardwick). Any information provided by the consultant that is passed onto performers or other members of the team or that appears in the final production will be mediated through the individual with whom the consultant spoke; indeed, Taplin has written that, of his lengthy discussions with Mitchell, 'much of this, I have to say—including much that I consider important—left no trace in the eventual production, at least not so far as I could see' ('An academic' 17). The academic consultant in this model, then, remains at a distance from the final output.

Another element of the consultant's role that Taplin outlines is verifying the accuracy of information, particularly in terms of how closely the chosen translation resembles the original Greek text. The production directed by Mitchell used a version of the plays by Ted Hughes selected by National Theatre Artistic Director Trevor Nunn; Hughes had died in October 1998.[5] In discussing Mitchell's engagement with Hughes' text, Taplin notes:

> I did work out that he was working primarily from Vellacott's Penguin [rather than the original Greek text]—I won't say he was working exclusively from that. The only time that came up was when … if something looked worth following and Katie Mitchell would say 'what about making something of this?' when I knew it was something which had no equivalent in the original. All I could say was well, that doesn't have any equivalent in the original. That is no way a prohibition of making something out of it because she wasn't working with the original she was working with a translation. But I suppose it was a factor for her to know whether or not it was in the original.
>
> (Hardwick)

Taplin's comments underline both the layers of mediation that tend to exist between modern theatre makers and the ancient text, and the emphasis that is so often placed on 'the original' in these productions. Taplin emphasises that the existence of a particular element in the translation but not the original text should not preclude the director from pursuing it in the production but does seem to suggest that knowing whether or not that element exists in the ancient text is important—or was at least for Katie Mitchell. Indeed, Taplin makes clear his belief that academic grounding for such productions is important:

> I have heard a director say—a rather good director, certainly a famous one—say, 'I just am not interested in what this play meant in 5th century Greece. It's of no interest to me whatsoever, I'm interested in what it means now.' There are some serious flaws in that attitude but that is what was said.
>
> (Hardwick)

Taplin suggests, then, that directors *should* be interested in the ancient meaning and context of Greek tragedies, and that academic consultants are one conduit for such information. Taken as a whole, Taplin's comments propose a model of the academic consultant as a person who can provide expert knowledge of the ancient text, its themes, and original context; such knowledge can be provided to the director outside of a rehearsal context for mediation to the rest of the creative team; and directors have a choice what information to make use of, and retain all of the creative control in the project, though they should at least pay attention to the academic input even if it is ultimately laid aside in the creative process.

The method Taplin describes is certainly not unique to himself, and it does have potential benefits. Professional theatre makers having the final say over the choices made in a professional theatre production is, clearly, preferable to those choices being made by a Classics academic. Nevertheless, the drawback of this method is its maintenance of a distinction between academic knowledge and theatrical knowledge: particularly, a sense of these two types of knowledge being in conflict. The classicist becomes a repository of information, with an emphasis on facts and accuracy, or otherwise authoritative and 'educated' interpretation; this is placed in contrast to a director's desire to, for example, make the play more relevant to a contemporary audience. If the consultant has contact only with the director or translator, there may arise a sense that academic knowledge is somehow inaccessible or inappropriate for other members of the creative team to consider or use. And if the consultant has minimal engagement in the development and rehearsal process—if the provision of academic knowledge is, essentially, a one-off and a one-way street—then opportunities for Classics academics to learn in turn from theatre makers are reduced. The consultant may be prompted to think about the *theory* of performance and may consider how their input is transformed (or not) into a performed outcome; but in a model of co-creation, there is potential for much richer engagement with the *practices* of performance.

Towards Co-creation

Some recent theatrical productions have modelled other ways of working. For the National Theatre's 2014 production of *Medea*, Lucy Jackson worked as academic consultant. In discussing the collaborative process of development, she notes that 'as testament to the openness of the room, one can also adduce the fact that I as an academic was allowed to sit in on the rehearsals to learn more about the process of staging ancient tragedy today' (108). For Jackson, taking part in rehearsals was the most productive part of her role, and she characterises her experience as primarily one of learning rather than imparting knowledge, even though she also prepared supplementary informational material for the production, notably an online exhibition about Greek drama in the United Kingdom and at the National Theatre ('Medea'). She seems to have been engaged in knowledge exchange, rather than acting as a repository of knowledge. Another model explored in depth in this volume is *Fragments* by Potential Difference: as Laura Swift, the academic member of that team, writes, 'My role was not an academic consultant but an equal co-creator; similarly, the artists involved should be understood as co-researchers of the academic ideas' (Swift, this volume 114). Swift's role was not as an external source of knowledge to be used or disregarded by the creative team as they saw fit; rather, she was fully engaged in the process from start to finish, on equal terms with the theatre makers.[6] Swift's experience directly impacted her view of the value of different types of knowledge in staging Greek tragedy today: 'working in a process that broke down traditional barriers between "academic expert" and "practitioner" allowed me to revisit assumptions about how expertise is created and shared' (Swift, this volume 122). This is also reflective of my experiences as a member of By Jove Theatre Company (now Theatre of the Gentle Furies), with whom I have worked for 11 years.

I was a founding member of By Jove and have been embedded in the company (primarily as a dramaturg) ever since. However, it is only since 2017 that I have conceptualised this work as part of my academic career, rather than a separate interest. This crystallised most significantly with the company's work on a project examining the myths of Orestes and queer identities, which culminated in the digital installation *The Gentlest Work* in 2021. By Jove works as a collective: productions are developed collaboratively and, while someone will often take a directorial role and writers may be named in the final production, shows are 'owned' creatively by all parties involved. This means that dramaturgs, directors, writers, performers, musicians, and choreographers are all on the same footing—as is anyone else who is brought into the room, such as an academic. Everyone is expected to take part in all rehearsal and development activities, if they are able to, whether physical or discussion-based. In this way of working, there can be no 'consultation': you are either a member of the team, sharing ideas democratically with others, or you are outside of the production.

Having worked with By Jove as a dramaturg, I was used to this way of working, but Nancy Rabinowitz, who first brought the idea of a project exploring the relationship between Orestes and Pylades to the company, was not. She described her role in the production process as follows:

> When it came to the adaptation process, I kept doing research, but I never really did get into writing anything for the performance piece. I think that, for me, it was so exciting not to be doing research for publication, and it was very liberating. I've taught reception for many years—when I teach tragedy, I don't just teach the ancient plays—but I hadn't really tried my hand at it, and I still haven't. I did get up and take part in the workshops, so there's hope for me yet! I would say that my role as spectator was to see where this material went with other people's interests at the helm, and allowing myself not to care what people did with what I had been working on, which is very different from an editing process or other kind of academic collaboration.
>
> (Bell et al.)

My own role was one of co-creation to a greater extent. By Jove worked on the project gradually, from 2018–2021. Workshops were held periodically with all participants, where a range of ideas (including academic ones) would be presented; all team members would then go away and allow these ideas to percolate, before returning to the next workshop ready to develop the ideas further. David Bullen has described the company's working process as one that 'de-centers one vision, whether that is from a director or a single writer (new or old) and helps us make work collaboratively' (Rabinowitz and Bullen 198). In this way, academic thinking became enmeshed with other concepts, and the idea of being able to trace any particular idea to any one member of the team broke down; as concepts for the finished work fell into place, the team felt a sense of collective ownership over them.

This way of working allowed for the democratisation of knowledge—for understanding stemming from academic study (of Classics or another discipline), professional training, and lived experience to be held in equal value— and for all participants to explore any mode of expression that appealed to them. The creative practitioners in the project were encouraged to offer their own interpretations of the characters and stories with which we were working; as the project was interested in viewing the myths through a queer lens, these interpretations often reflected the deeply personal experiences of the artists. These interpretations and ways of knowing the myth were held as no less valid than the canonical, academic interpretations. Conversely, in this environment I was empowered to explore my understanding of the myth not only through academic enquiry but through creative writing. This was a vulnerable experience: I had never shared any creative writing publicly. But the nature of the working process, in which all ideas were welcome and everything went 'into the pot' for people to react to as they chose, meant that the pressure to produce polished writing was reduced, and instead I felt able to share alongside the more experienced writers in the room. In the same way, my academic reflections equally went 'into the pot': they were not privileged because of my educational background but were simply considered another useful form of input into the creative process.

The final installation brought together dozens of texts, images, audio and video recordings that created a multiplicity of voices and viewpoints telling the stories of Orestes and his family. Among the pieces produced by seasoned creatives were poems and creative reflections produced by Nancy Rabinowitz and me. Equally included were the analyses and insights of non-academics into the myth and the scholarship surrounding it. The presentation of creative and academic work, co-produced by creatives and academics, in a non-hierarchical way seemed to me to undo a sense of the academic as a repository of authoritative knowledge and instead suggested that the stories of Greek tragedy can be understood in multiple, equally valuable ways simultaneously. There was no sense of the 'correct' interpretation, as in the case of Murray, or of 'fact-checking' against the originals as in Taplin's reflections; rather, the project allowed us to unpick some of the ways in which Classics academia seeks to legitimise and verify knowledge about the ancient world and made space for valuing a range of ways of knowing and understanding ancient stories.

Conclusion

When an academic consultant is employed for a production of Greek tragedy and remains at a distance from the creative process—particularly a high-profile consultant, and even more so one who has consulted on productions before—a hierarchy of knowledge is established that emphasises concepts of authority and authenticity. The presence of a consultant suggests that the creative team on the production do not have access to enough knowledge from the script and from their own expertise and research to successfully produce the play; it suggests, in fact, that Greek tragedy cannot be understood by just anyone, but requires specialist knowledge. It is necessary to consult an authority, an expert: someone who has closely studied ancient drama, who has perhaps published scholarly works on the topic, and who is able to enlighten the members of the production team who do not have such knowledge. Although the experience of the consultant may differ, the relationship of the consultant to the production is designed to be one-way: the consultant delivers knowledge, which is either integrated into the production or rejected by the creative team. The consultant may hope to learn something about modern theatre or about the reception of ancient drama but is not expected to develop their understanding of Greek tragedy. This is not necessarily an imposition by the consultant—their input is often requested by the director, and the nature of the relationship dictated by the director—or a conscious devaluing of their own knowledge by the creative team: rather, it is a symptom of the way the Classics ecology has operated in the United Kingdom, with classical knowledge perceived to be something difficult and held only by an (elite) few. The fact that academic consultants are often drawn from the Universities of Oxford and Cambridge, and that the same consultants are used again and again, reinforces this perception.[7]

This model of the authority of the consultant connects closely to an idea of authenticity that is often associated with Greek tragedy: the sense that some original, 'true' way of performing a Greek tragic play exists, and that with enough knowledge, a modern production might come close to it.[8] The presentation of authenticity often manifests in the use of masks, staging resembling ancient Athenian stagecraft, the use of song and dance particularly for the chorus, actors playing multiple roles, or even the prominent use of an ancient poet's name in marketing materials even when the play being produced is a fairly loose adaptation: see, for example, the National Theatre's *Phaedra* (2023), marketed as a new play 'after Euripides, Seneca and Racine' ('*Phaedra*'). Even when the input of consultants is rejected, this is often framed as an active choice to step away from 'authenticity' for creative purposes—for example, to make the play more appealing to modern audiences, for whom the conventions of Greek tragedy might be unfamiliar and alienating. The association of Classics with ideas of authenticity is, as with authority, not limited to the context of consultants on popular productions of Greek tragedy: for example, a desire for authenticity pervades media outcry when universities are reported to no longer be teaching particular classical authors—often Homer and Virgil—to the same extent or, crucially, in the original language. Indeed, more politically radical reimaginings of Greek tragedy (and other ancient sources) draw much of their power from this sense of (co-opted) authenticity and authority (see, for example, Komporaly 13–19). But by replicating these associations, whether consciously or not, major productions that use high-profile classical consultants in a way that is distanced from the creative process continue to suggest that classical knowledge is something held by only a few, that Greek drama cannot be properly understood without a consideration—whether embraced or rejected—of its original performance context, and that this knowledge and understanding is something desirable.

The model of co-creation that we see in projects like *Fragments* and *The Gentlest Work*, however, is one that puts the 'authority' of the classicist in the mix as an ingredient along with the authority of theatre makers, the authority of lived experience of practitioners, and other kinds of authority to the extent that hierarchies are broken down among these groups and there is no longer an attempt to speak to, either positively or negatively, an authentic original. Rather, there is a freedom to work within a set of story paradigms and cultural contexts that can be put to whatever use the team wishes. When this happens, the resulting production is likely to be less recognisable as 'Greek tragedy', but in being so may help to demonstrate that the ancient world does not have to be something distant or elitist, and that understanding ancient texts and concepts is of equal value to other types of understanding. The Classics academic embedded in the development process as a co-creator must be both careful not to assert their knowledge as authoritative, and willing to open themselves up to more creative processes and ways of knowing than they may be used to. If this can happen, the resulting process can be deeply rewarding for all involved and can also produce theatrical and academic work that is innovative and impactful.

Notes

1. On processes of translation for the modern stage, see Macintosh, 'Theater Translation'.
2. For an in-depth discussion of the strategies used by Murray in his translation of *Bacchae* to convey his ideas about the play, see Perris (59–78).
3. Data extracted from the Archive of Performances of Greek and Roman Drama catalogue, http://www.apgrd.ox.ac.uk/research-collections. Accessed 21 July 2023.
4. On Harrison's translation, see Taplin, 'The Harrison Version' as well as Latham.
5. See discussion of Mitchell's work at the National Theatre in Bullen, *Greek Tragedy*.
6. Notably, in an article for *The Stage*, Kate Maltby overlooks the co-created nature of *Fragments* and centres Swift as (sole) author, despite publicity for the play indicating otherwise (Maltby). This is indicative of expectations about the roles academics have had and should have in producing theatre: Maltby also mentions the more common role of academics as 'literary advisers' and suggests that academic involvement beyond this level is unusual.

7 On the predominance of these two universities in both the Classics and theatre ecologies, see Bullen, this volume.
8 The idea of achieving authenticity in staging Greek tragedy, in coming close to its 'origin myth', is raised by Laera, 'Reaching Athens' and explored in depth in Laera, *Reaching Athens*.

Works Cited

Bell, Marcus, et al. 'The Orestes Project.' *Practitioners' Voices in Classical Reception Studies* 11 (2020), www.open.ac.uk/arts/research/pvcrs/2020/orestesproject. Accessed 1 Aug. 2023.

Bullen, David. 'Dionysus the New Woman: Maenadic and Feminist Intersections in Lillah McCarthy's 1908 Bacchae.' *Theatre Notebook* 75.1 (2021): 51–70.

———. *Greek Tragedy as Twenty-first Century British Theatre: Why, What, How*. Liverpool University Press, forthcoming.

Croall, Jonathan. *Peter Hall's Bacchai: The National Theatre at Work*. Oberon Books, 2007.

'Fragments.' *Potential Difference*, 2023, www.potentialdifference.org.uk/productions/fragments. Accessed 1 Aug. 2023.

Hall, Edith. 'Tony Harrison as Founder of Classical Reception Studies.' *Tony Harrison and the Classics*, edited by Sandie Byrne, Oxford University Press, 2022, 29–56.

Hall, Edith, and Fiona Macintosh. *Greek Tragedy and the British Theatre 1660–1914*. Oxford University Press, 2005.

Hardwick, Lorna. 'Oliver Taplin, Academic, Translator and Writer, in Interview with Lorna Hardwick (Magdalen College, Oxford, 30th June 2008).' *Practitioners' Voices in Classical Reception Studies* 2 (2010), www.open.ac.uk/arts/research/pvcrs/2010/taplin. Accessed 1 Aug. 2023.

Jackson, Lucy. 'Forces at Work: Euripides' *Medea* at the National Theatre 2014.' *Adapting Translation for the Stage*, edited by Geraldine Brodie and Emma Cole, Routledge, 2017, 104–117.

Komporaly, Jozefina. *Radical Revival as Adaptation: Theatre, Politics, Society*. Palgrave Macmillan, 2017.

Laera, Margherita. 'Reaching Athens: Performing Participation and Community in Rimini Protokoll's *Prometheus in Athens*.' *Performance Research* 16.4 (2011): 46–51.

———. *Reaching Athens: Community, Democracy and Other Mythologies in Adaptations of Greek Tragedy*. Peter Lang, 2013.

Latham, Caroline. 'The Sound of the *Oresteia*.' *Tony Harrison and the Classics*, edited by Sandie Byrne, Oxford University Press, 2022, 247–266.

Macintosh, Fiona. 'From the Court to the National: The Theatrical Legacy of Gilbert Murray's Bacchae.' *Gilbert Murray Reassessed: Hellenism, Theatre, and International Politics*, edited by Christopher Stray, Oxford University Press, 2007, 145–166.

———. 'Theater Translation and Performance.' *Encyclopedia of Ancient Greek Language and Linguistics*, edited by Georgios K. Giannakis, Brill, 2014.

Maltby, Kate. 'Teachable Moments: Why Theatre Should Open Its Arms to Academics.' *The Stage*, 6 June 2023, www.thestage.co.uk/opinion/teachable-moments-why-theatre-should-open-its-arms-to-academics. Accessed 1 Aug. 2023.

'Medea.' *The Oxford Research Centre in the Humanities*, www.torch.ox.ac.uk/medea?filter-3626-project-825261=26491. Accessed 1 Aug. 2023.

Morwood, James. 'Gilbert Murray's Translations of Greek Tragedy.' *Gilbert Murray Reassessed: Hellenism, Theatre, and International Politics*, edited by Christopher Stray, Oxford University Press, 2007, 133–144.

Parker, R. B. 'The National Theatre's *Oresteia*, 1981–82.' *Greek Tragedy and Its Legacy: Essays Presented to D. J. Conacher*, edited by Martin Cropp, et al., University of Calgary Press, 1986, 337–357.

Perris, Simon. *The Gentle, Jealous God: Reading Euripides' Bacchae in English*. Bloomsbury, 2016.

'Phaedra.' *National Theatre*, 2023, www.nationaltheatre.org.uk/productions/phaedra. Accessed 1 Aug. 2023.

Rabinowitz, Nancy Sorkin, and David Bullen. '*Iphigenia in Tauris: Iphigenia and Artemis? Reading Queer/Performing Queer*.' *Queer Euripides: Re-readings in Greek Tragedy*, edited by Sarah Olsen and Mario Telò, Bloomsbury, 2022, 197–206.

Taplin, Oliver. 'An Academic in the Rehearsal Room.' *Greek and Roman Drama: Translation and Performance*, edited by John Barsby, Verlag J. B. Metzler, 2002, 7–22.

———. 'The Harrison Version: "So Long Ago That it's Become a Song?"' *Agamemnon in Performance 458 B.C. to A.D. 2004*, edited by Fiona Macintosh, et al., Oxford University Press, 2005, 235–251.

'Theatre by Edith Hall.' *Edith Hall*, www.edithhall.co.uk/theatre. Accessed 1 Aug. 2023.

3 Between Actors and Archons

Mediating Knowledges of Greek Tragedy in/as Performance

David Bullen

'In my experience', wrote Michael Billington in 2009, 'actors often have a deeper understanding of plays ... than many critics and academics'. Billington cites Simon Russell Beale's description of acting as 'three-dimensional literary criticism' ('Simon Russell Beale is no Shakespearean fool'). But when it comes to Greek tragedy, I have often spoken to theatre makers, especially actors, about their work with these texts only for them to preface their comments with a disavowal of their knowledge: they know nothing, they say, because they are 'not a classicist', or words to that effect. Even an esteemed actor like Vanessa Redgrave turned to a classicist, Simon Goldhill, when she was due to play Hecuba in 2005; vexed by her director, she sought help from someone deemed as *really* knowing the material. Goldhill was initially not sure what to offer, because a 'literary critical argument' was not really what was required—and so he set out to address the gap himself (1). But his subsequent book, *How to Stage Greek Tragedy Today*, is explicitly not a how-to manual (4), and turns back instead to the 'three-dimensional literary criticism' of actors, as well the practice of directors, writers, and other modern theatre artists. The theatre maker turned to the classicist, but because Classics did not (all) have the answers, the classicist turned back to the theatre makers.

There are two categories of person poised as 'knowing' Greek tragedy: the academic/classicist and the theatre maker. Clearly, they know the material in different ways, and as such the knowledge they possess of Greek tragedy is different. Many of the chapters in this volume explore the reciprocal benefits of, to use the term favoured in UK higher education at present, knowledge exchange between academics and theatre makers.[1] Christine Plastow points to early 20th-century exchanges that helped to establish Greek tragedies as performable plays on the British stage, and subsequent exchanges between academics and artists. Histories of Greek tragedy *in* performance are thus shaped by flows and exchanges of knowledge(s) about Greek tragedy *as* performance. As Stephe Harrop—amongst a number of authors in Harrop and Hall's ground-breaking 2010 volume *Theorising Performance*—makes clear, there are no fixed answers to the question of 'how to stage Greek tragedy today'; rather, each new instance of practice is a new process of negotiation

DOI: 10.4324/b22844-4

between different kinds of knowers and their knowledges.[2] I see this as aligned to the broader concept of ecology as suggested in this volume. But as Christine Plastow and I discuss in the introduction, this is complicated by a hierarchy amongst knowers of the ancient Greek and Roman worlds that emerges from the historically privileged position of a discipline called Classics that lays claim to knowledge of these worlds, something reflected in the adjective 'classical', as in classical world or classical plays.

Goldhill's book provides an example. He structures his discussion around problems he identifies that he suggests are presented by Greek tragedy. In each chapter Goldhill proceeds from a discussion of the ancient world to analysing theatre makers' 'successes and failures' in trying to 'solve these difficulties in the theatre' (2). The book is thus underpinned by a conviction that 'the ancient world will reveal again and again essential insights' (5), which prefigures a concluding assertion that Greek tragedy is 'the foundation and origin of Western theatre' in part because of its capacity to 'inspire, challenge, and fulfil artists and audiences' (222). In this way, Goldhill positions the ancient world as orienting modern practice—the latter's source, compass, and aspirational paradigm—and the expert classicist as arbiter of the 'success' of theatre makers, who are rendered non-experts attempting to solve the 'problem' that is Greek tragedy. Greek tragedy in modern performance is thus conceived of as a history of attempts at reviving what was once so brilliantly alive in the 5th-century BCE. Consequently, Greek tragedy as modern performance becomes a set of problems to be resolved that are established by the (assumptions of) originary greatness located firmly in the texts and in the ways they were first staged; that greatness can be revived in the present if the theatre makers pass the tests the texts set them; and it is classicists who serve as guides to how to pass the test and assessors of whether the tests are passed.

This is not to dismiss the value of Goldhill's book. In her review, Fiona Macintosh praised Goldhill's displacement of Aristotle's prevailing influence in his emphasis on tragedy as a genre of conflict ('Move over, Aristotle'). This has influenced later academic-practitioners, including Zachary Dunbar and Stephe Harrop in their *Greek Tragedy and the Contemporary Actor*, which I will return to in my conclusion. I know that, when first approaching Greek tragedy as a theatre maker, I found Goldhill's book immensely helpful, because there are aspects of Greek tragedy that differ substantially from other dramatic forms and Goldhill's elucidation of these differences can inform what approach to take. It is because of the book's value that I draw attention to its hierarchising of knowledges. Such books are mechanisms by which knowledges of Greek tragedy in and as performance, developed through exchanges between academics and artists, are mediated. I am interested in this mediation and how it is possible for the knowledge generated and held by artists—especially actors—to be made visible as equally significant when it comes to contemporary understanding of the performance possibilities afforded by Greek tragedy.

It is easy for a slippage to occur when thinking about theatre makers that equates the work of a director or writer with that of an actor. The latter's labour is more visible and more ephemeral: it is through actors' bodies that a performance is realised, but because knowledge of their craft is inseparable from those bodies, it makes it easy for it to become muddled up with more lasting performance traces with which it is entangled, most prominently text. For academics, who are often in the position of mediating knowledge—especially when it comes to Greek tragedy—it is possible to watch an actor perform and describe this performance, but the academic transmits only an impression of the knowledge being generated and held by the actor. It is possible for the actor's knowledge to be transmitted, but it can only happen through doing, the transfer of practices and techniques from one body to another, as occurs in practical classes in UK HE drama departments and conservatoires (Harrop discusses this further in her chapter in this volume). The important point here is that when an actor comes to work with Greek tragedy, realising words in body and voice, the knowledge about Greek tragedy as performance that they generate is not rooted in much to do with the ancient world but rather in lineages of modern practices and techniques, as well as prior acting and life experiences. This will vary from actor to actor, but even someone who has no training or professional acting experience will draw on the experience of being in the world today. As director Kwame Owusu remarked to me following his experience of working with trainee actors on an adaptation of *Bacchae*, the actor interprets text, no matter its canonical weight, through the prism of their perception of the present world. For Owusu, the 'actors are our specialists' (Bullen).

My thinking here draws on performance studies scholar Diana Taylor's conceptualisation of how knowledge is transferred in *The Archive and the Repertoire* (2003), though I am adapting it to a very different context. Like Taylor, I am concerned with embodied knowledge. Taylor employs 'archive' and 'repertoire' as concepts, where the former refers to knowledge that exists as objects (texts, archaeological remains, etc.) and is thus abstracted from the knower (19), and the latter 'enacts embodied memory: performances, gestures, orality, movement, dance, singing—in short all those acts usually thought of as ephemeral, nonreproducible knowledge'. The repertoire thus 'requires presence: people participate in the production and reproduction of knowledge by "being there," being a part of the transmission' (20). And unlike the relative stability of the archive's materials, the knowledge in the repertoire transforms through interpretation by successive knowers.

Academics, especially those engaged with the ancient world, principally deal in the archival, both in the use of literal archives and in the emphasis on the generation and transfer of knowledge via written texts; the defining criterion of a PhD is the creation of new knowledge, partly or wholly assessed through a written dissertation. Actors, meanwhile, acquire, generate, and transfer their knowledge mainly through embodied experience. As mediators of knowledge of Greek tragedy, therefore, academics often occupy a privileged position. As Jacques Derrida recalls, 'archive' has its origins in ancient Greece in the house of the archon, a governing magistrate in the city-state, where official documents were kept. For Derrida this evokes the foundational connection between archives and power: the archon both governs access to the archive's documents and has the authority to interpret the contents, and so the documents acquire authoritative status (10). An academic such as Goldhill might be seen as archon in relation to the archive of Greek tragedy and its uses in performance, wielding authority as both keeper and interpreter. Goldhill's example is particularly pertinent in terms of thinking about the power dynamics of the archive because of the 'house' of this archon: the University of Cambridge, which alongside Oxford plays a major role in mediating knowledge not just of Greek tragedy but of theatre through a combination of its cultural positioning and reciprocal exchanges within its own networks.[3] The archive is implicated in the control of knowledge, and, in this sense, the archontic role of the academic and academic institution in relation to archival knowing means that they have significant power as knowledge mediators, especially when they operate from positions of such cultural prominence as Oxbridge. Although some actors (not least Redgrave) also enjoy cultural prominence, many do not. The academic-as-archon and the actor are not binary oppositions that map onto archive and repertoire—in any case, as Taylor states, these categories operate in a 'constant state of interaction' (21). My intention here is therefore not to valorise the repertoire over and against the archive. Rather, I want to highlight some examples in which knowledges of Greek tragedy in and as performance are mediated, paying attention to how they configure the knowledge of actors and other artists in relation to the archival knowledge and the archontic role of academics in keeping and interpreting that knowledge.

*

My first example is the Archive of Performances of Greek and Roman Drama (APGRD), founded by Edith Hall and Oliver Taplin in 1996 at the University of Oxford. Alongside Fiona Macintosh, who joined in 2000 and was director from 2010 to 2024, the impact of these three scholars and the APGRD has been enormous—concurrent with, and influencing, turns towards theatre history, reception, and performance in the study of Greek tragedy. The centre functions as a literal archive in that it holds collections of materials and maintains an extraordinary database of 9,000 productions that make use of, in some way, ancient Greek and Roman drama.[4] In Taylor's sense of the archival, the APGRD is unparalleled in the knowledge it holds of Greek tragedy in performance. But in Macintosh and Giovanna Di Martino's account, as early as 2005 the team at the APGRD have wrestled with the 'pitfalls and problems of the archival process' (234). This has included resistance to the problematic dynamics that Derrida attributes to the archive, and in seeking multiple associations with practitioners and academics from beyond Classics (and beyond Oxford), the APGRD has become a site of exchange between the differing knowledges.

Macintosh has positioned the APGRD as 're-opening' in step with the 'contextual turn' in archive theory, aligning its function with former National Theatre archivist Gavin Clarke's description of the archive as the 'engine room' of an organisation that facilitates the 'regular interchange of ideas' (Macintosh 268, 274; cf. Macintosh and Di Martino 235–236).[5] I read Macintosh's contextualising of the APGRD's practice as manifesto as much as historiography: if Macintosh is the archon of this archive, then under her direction there were ongoing attempts to re-think dynamics of access and meaning-making. The APGRD's approach to publication—which was pathbreaking early on (see, e.g., Hall and Macintosh; Hall, Macintosh, and Wrigley; Hall, Macintosh, and Taplin; Macintosh et al.)—has recently changed through the creation of free interactive ebooks. In this way the paradigmatic form of archival knowledge transfer, the book, is animated with a 'sense of liveness' that, so Macintosh and Di Martino report, has made them amenable to use in actor training (241). This is one innovative example of how the APGRD mediates knowledges of Greek tragedy in ways that forestall the hegemony of archival knowing and the attendant archontic authority that can become attached to academics as 'proper' knowers of these plays; instead, archival knowledge is able to flow in ways that both recognises the knowledge of artists and makes space for artists as equitable knowers. This is seen further in a 40-minute film co-produced by the APGRD and The Oxford Research Centre for the Humanities (TORCH) in which director Paul O'Mahony and two actors, Evelyn Miller and Tim Delap, rehearse a scene from *Antigone*.[6] The intention was to document the messy, multi-bodied knowledge creation/transfer that occurs in the rehearsal room. Such documentation is not the same as the knowledge that was in circulation in the rehearsal room (cf. Taylor 20) but what the APGRD seem to be doing is attempting to resist the displacement of actors' embodied knowledge and knowledge-making that can occur when performance is 'read' as 'text' by drawing attention to 'the craft and process of acting and the role of the rehearsal in the creation of a play-text's meanings' (Macintosh and Di Martino 246).

Macintosh's role at the APGRD has informally been described as akin to a theatre producer by default (Macintosh, interview). This might be a helpful means of reconceptualising the 'archonship' of someone in Macintosh's position—less a privileged keeper-interpreter than a facilitator of meaningful knowledge exchange. This aligns with Macintosh's identification of the APGRD as akin to the National's 'engine room' archive; in this and other ways—Macintosh also describes the APGRD in its early years as Oxford's *de facto* theatre department (Macintosh, 'Museums' 276)—there is a repositioning of the APGRD as closer to an arts organisation than a research centre in an academic Classics department. On the one hand, it is not an arts organisation, and it is important to note such an identity formed in the context of Oxford's reluctance to acknowledge theatre-making as a legitimate means of knowledge production or subject of academic enquiry (although this has changed with the foundation of TORCH and the new Schwarzman Centre's Humanities Cultural Programme). In this sense, the APGRD's knowledge mediation exists in the shadow of, in Macintosh and Di Martino's words, 'an elitist discipline and an elitist university' (234).

On the other hand, this identity as quasi-arts organisation is precisely what has enabled knowledge exchange between academics and artists to flourish. Macintosh has played an important role, but she has not worked alone: the APGRD has an advisory board that includes theatre makers, and its programmes have meant that artists, many of whom come from outside of Classics, have been a constant presence in what might otherwise be an academic space defined by the discipline.[7] Macintosh emblematises this: her background is not originally in Classics and from the beginning of her time in the discipline in the early 1990s, her capacity to assume a 'different identity' enabled her to ask questions that were otherwise not being asked and to make connections beyond the field, such as with theatre historian David Wiles; this led, ultimately, to Macintosh's arrival at the APGRD in 2000 (interview). But it goes beyond Macintosh and is perhaps most acutely visible in the Onassis Programme (2005–2011), led by theatre maker Helen Eastman, that produced new work in the United Kingdom that included Yaël Farber's South African *Oresteia*, *Molora* (one of Macintosh's proudest achievements, interview). It is also visible in the ongoing annual postgraduate symposium convened between the APGRD and the Department of Drama, Theatre, and Dance at Royal Holloway, which has fostered generations of new academics and academic-practitioners from across the world in multiple fields. This includes me, and so this chapter and volume is, to some extent, part of the APGRD's extended impact as a knowledge mediator.

My second example is theatre company Actors of Dionysus (styled lowercase as aod), founded in 1993 by writer and academic David Stuttard. Actor Tamsin Shasha soon joined Stuttard and became sole artistic director in 2003 when he left. Over the last 30 years their work has ranged across the United Kingdom and abroad in over 40 productions, the majority of which have toured. As with the APGRD, I have a relationship to aod: I have been a trustee since 2017. Even so, it is simply a fact that there is no other company in the United Kingdom with as much experience of working with ancient Greek drama. What distinguishes aod as knowledge mediators, though, is their educational programme. The company's education lead Mark Katz estimates aod has delivered, on average, 30 school workshops on Greek tragedy per year for the last 20 years, with a total of around 12,000 participants from across the United Kingdom.[8] Crucially, the knowledge imparted by Shasha and Katz, who deliver almost all the workshops, comes from, and is transferred via, what might be conceptualised as something approaching

Taylor's concept of repertoire. They have come to know Greek tragedy as performance through their professional training and staging experiences, not through academic study, though via Stuttard the latter has been an influence on their creative output. They have passed on that knowledge to generations of workshop participants through practice. It can only be speculated as to how many participants of an aod workshop have passed the knowledge on to others through subsequent creative practice in educational, amateur, or professional contexts or else through becoming teachers—certainly, the company attests to instances in which academics and artists working in the United Kingdom have said that their interest in, and understanding of, Greek tragedy began with an aod workshop (Shasha, Ruddiman, and Katz).

Katz trained at the Academy of Live and Recorded Arts; Shasha trained at the Oxford School of Drama, the École Philippe Gaulier, and the National Centre for Circus Arts. The pair have also trained in, or experienced through work with other artists, the practices of Complicité, Jacques Lecoq, Michael Chekhov, and Augusto Boal (Shasha, Ruddiman, and Katz). This informs both the company's creative practice and educational work—as Katz remarked to me, 'elements of workshops appear in our productions and the productions themselves have led to workshops using elements of the rehearsal process' (Shasha, Ruddiman, and Katz). The knowledge being transferred in aod's workshops, therefore, is precisely the knowledge aod use to stage Greek tragedy. It situates them within wider lineages of theatre-making practices that have been used to engage with Greek tragedy.[9] To understand aod as knowledge mediators it is essential to attend to these modern influences as much as it is the ancient material they work with, because it is these influences that shaped their not inconsiderable reach over the last three decades: in addition to the reach of their workshops, the company estimates that their productions have been seen by perhaps as many as 750,000 people.[10]

aod's knowledge mediation may be primarily through repertoire, but they have also tried to make their knowledge visible via archival means. It is not a coincidence that this began with Stuttard, an academic and teacher at a school in St Andrew's at the time of company's founding. In this sense, their engagement with ancient Greek drama may have been shaped by modern theatre practices, but it has always been a product of the Classics ecology: prominent classicists contributed to essay volumes published by aod, which have as their successor Stuttard's popular *Looking at* series of academic essays attached to his translations.[11] Academics, including those instrumental to the APGRD such as Taplin, Hall, and Macintosh, also frequently gave pre-show talks at aod shows. The company have always sought to articulate their claim to knowing Greek tragedy through association with Classics academics in their archontic function as perceived keepers of knowledge concerning the ancient Greek world—one of the first things Shasha mentioned in our interview was that aod's first production received high praise from Kenneth Dover (Shasha, Ruddiman, and Katz). Dover's remark is on aod's website on a page peppered with such comments from classicists and academic institutions such as the Classical Association. Under Shasha, this has shifted to the courting of public figures associated with Classics, such as Bettany Hughes and Natalie Haynes. This functions as an effective marketing strategy for a fringe company with limited resources, helping them to become integral to the Classics ecology in spite of their marginality in the related theatre ecology. This ecological embeddedness became especially clear during Covid lockdowns in the United Kingdom, when aod started their social media 'Daily Dose'. While this initially involved Shasha reading passages (in translation) from ancient Greek and Roman texts, it has grown so that a range of figures—including Classics academics and students as well as celebrities such as Stephen Fry—have contributed.[12] The wide circulation of these videos rendered aod a crux in a public network of those interested in the ancient Greek and Roman worlds, at least during that time. This contributes to aod's profile as a knowledge mediator, but it is not without drawbacks. From my vantage point as a trustee, I have seen how the company's work (especially the Daily Dose) has contributed to 'save (the) Classics' discourses that have a tendency towards the idealisation of Greek tragic texts' supposedly universal value. Moreover, seeking validation through Classics and classicists risks an implicit understanding of the company's work as somehow lacking in legitimacy without the seal of approval from those who 'really know' Greek tragedy.

*

This chapter is ultimately another addition to archival knowledge, but I hope the key takeaway will be the importance of attending to the knowledge held by theatre makers, which may differ in kind from the knowledge of the academic (especially in the case of the actor), and to their role as knowledge mediators. But just as Taylor emphasises that the repertoire does not automatically challenge the hegemonic potential of the archive (22), the knowledge mediation of theatre makers can uphold the hierarchical precedence of academic knowledge. aod's work has sometimes been innovative, especially in the period following Stuttard's departure—Shasha had long desired to be 'less faithful' in interpreting Greek drama (Shasha, Ruddiman, and Katz)—but it has not been especially radical. In broadly following a vision of Greek tragedy developed by Classics academics, established by Stuttard but persisting under Shasha, the company has cultivated a niche with schools as purveyors of practical knowledge that will help students reaffirm that vision, precisely because the vision has also shaped GCSE and A level syllabi. This is Goldhill's problem-solving approach in another form: Shasha and Katz may draw on their theatre-making knowledge in what they teach, but the appeal is still the provision of 'answers' to the 'problem' of performing Greek tragedy, the terms of which have been established by academics' archival orientation to the subject.

I want, therefore, to bookend the chapter with a mention of another text that mediates knowledge of Greek tragedy in/as modern performance, Zachary Dunbar and Stephe Harrop's *Greek Tragedy and the Contemporary Actor*. Dunbar and Harrop put actors on equal footing with the academic by making the former an explorer of meanings within a field of possibilities that are nuanced, rather than determined, by the kinds of texts constituting Greek tragedy and what is known of the associated performance culture. In this configuration, the question of how Greek tragedy informs modern performance is an open one. An emphasis on actors leaves meaning provisional, throwing open the possibility of who has authority to make meaning with Greek tragedy rather than assuming that this authority resides first with the academic and thus that theatre makers' task is to realise Greek tragedy's intrinsic meanings. It also helps resist assumptions of authorship that foreground writers and directors over other kinds of artists. Crucially, it makes visible the manner in which those in the present synthesise knowledge of the ancient Greek and Roman worlds with other experiences, interests, and traditions, and that this happens not just textually and intellectually but in the bodies of the actors. It is no coincidence that Dunbar and Harrop both have associations with the APGRD, and their book's approach is cognate with the APGRD's 're-opening' that acknowledges artists as experts in their own right and leaves space for meaningful knowledge exchange. aod, especially under Shasha, also point towards the potential for actors to have authority as makers and sharers of meaning when it comes to Greek tragedy, even if the company's efforts to validate its work through the archonship of Classics and classicists can undermine that authority. If the knowledge of actors and other artists can be valued for what it is, rather than seen as more or less successful illustrations of principles determined by academics, it has the potential to transform understanding of Greek tragedy both in and as modern performance. In unmooring the modern performance possibilities of Greek tragedy from a defining relationship to a lost original—in other words, the proper realisation of existing, if multifaceted, meanings—and proceeding instead from a position whereby theatre makers are acknowledged as crafting meaning from these patchy, provisional, and yet thematically rich texts, it becomes possible to better comprehend the complexities of how these texts (fail to) resonate in the present and of the varied knowledges and knowledge lineages that come to bear on them.

Notes

1 On knowledge exchange in which both Classics and theatre are implicated, see Cole.
2 The present chapter is indebted not only to Harrop's work here and elsewhere, but to many of the other contributions to that volume, as well as fruitful conversations with Harrop, Hall, Fiona Macintosh, Lucy Ruddiman, Tamsin Shasha, Christine Plastow, Lucy Jackson, Emma Cole, and many others.
3 See further the introduction to this volume.

4 See Macintosh as well as Macintosh and Di Martino.
5 On the 're-opening' of archives, see Macintosh 273–277, who cites articles by Cook and Nesmith.
6 The video is available at: www.youtube.com/watch?v=Y6Qi3RjODlk (accessed 1 Aug. 2023).
7 See www.apgrd.ox.ac.uk/about/programmes (accessed 1 Aug. 2023).
8 The participants have been a mix of Classics and drama students. The workshops are often delivered to state-maintained schools (sometimes for free, see Rogers) in regions experiencing 'Classics poverty' (Hunt and Holmes-Henderson).
9 Stephe Harrop's chapter in this volume identifies aod as one practitioner in the legacy of Lecoq-derived approaches to the chorus. For further discussion of approaches to Greek tragedy and their origins in modern theatre practices, see Eastman (on the chorus) and Dunbar and Harrop (on acting).
10 This is the figure given by Rogers, then the company's general manager. In our recent correspondence, however, Katz estimates a total audience of around 200,000.
11 Early aod publications included *An Introduction to Trojan Women* (1996), *Essays on Agamemnon* (2002), *Essays on Trojan Women* (2001), and *Essays on Bacchae* (2006). Stuttard's *Looking at* series (2010–) has, to date, volumes on *Lysistrata*, *Medea*, *Bacchae*, *Antigone*, *Ajax*, *Agamemnon*, and *Persians*.
12 The first 182 are viewable here: www.youtube.com/playlist?list=PLxxXqx1txVl4JJJ-QGq65gJ5gWAamnlGe (accessed 1 Aug. 2023).

Works Cited

Billington, Michael. 'Simon Russell Beale Is No Shakespearean Fool.' *The Guardian*, 22 June 2009, www.theguardian.com/stage/theatreblog/2009/jun/22/simon-russell-beale-shakespeare. Accessed 1 Aug. 2023.

Bullen, David. 'Kwame Owusu and Katherine Soper.' *Practitioners' Voices in Classical Reception Studies*. 15 (2024).

Cole, Emma. 'Knowledge Exchange and the Creative Industries: A Reflective Commentary on Current Practice.' *Research for All* 5.2 (2021): 194–204.

Cook, Terry. 'The Concept of the Archival Fonds in the Post-Custodial Era: Theory, Problems and Solutions.' *Archivaria* 35 (1993): 4–37.

Dunbar, Zachary, and Stephe Harrop. *Greek Tragedy and the Contemporary Actor*. Palgrave Macmillan, 2018.

Eastman, Helen. 'Chorus in Contemporary British Theatre.' *Choruses, Ancient and Modern*, edited by Joshua Billings, Felix Budelmann and Fiona Macintosh, Oxford University Press, 2013, 363–376.

Goldhill, Simon. *How to Stage Greek Tragedy Today*. University of Chicago Press, 2007.

Hall, Edith, and Fiona Macintosh. *Greek Tragedy and the British Theatre 1660–1914*. Oxford University Press, 2005.

Hall, Edith, Fiona Macintosh, and Oliver Taplin, editors. *Medea in Performance 1500–2000*. Legenda, 2000.

Hall, Edith, Macintosh, Fiona, and Amanda Wrigley, editors. *Dionysus Since 69: Greek Tragedy at the Dawn of the Third Millennium*. Oxford University Press, 2004.

Harrop, Stephe. 'Physical Performance and the Languages of Translation.' *Theorising Performance: Greek Drama, Cultural History and Critical Practice*, edited by Edith Hall and Stephe Harrop, Duckworth, 2010, 232–240.

Hunt, Steven, and Arlene Holmes-Henderson. 'A Level Classics Poverty: Classical Subjects in Schools in England: Access, Attainment and Progression.' *CUCD Bulletin* 50 (2021): 1–26.

Katz, Mark. 'aod Figures.' Received by David Bullen, 26 Sep. 2022.

Macintosh, Fiona. 'Move Over, Aristotle.' *Literary Review* 349 (2007).

———. 'Museums, Archives, and Collecting.' *The Cambridge Companion to Theatre History*, edited by David Wiles and Christine Dymkowski, Cambridge University Press, 2012, 267–280.

———. Personal interview. 25 Apr 2023.

Macintosh, Fiona, and Giovanna Di Martino. 'Archiving and Interpreting Greek and Roman Theatre: The Archive as Engine Room and Digital Hub.' *Futuro Classico* 7 (2021): 233–251.

Macintosh, Fiona, Michelakis, Pantelis, Edith Hall, and Oliver Taplin, editors. *Agamemnon in Performance 458 BC to AD 2004*. Oxford University Press, 2005.

Nesmith, Tom. 'Reopening the Archives: Bringing New Contextualities into Archival Theory and Practice.' *Archivaria* 60 (2005): 259–274.

Rogers, Megan. 'Actors of Dionysus.' *Journal of Classics Teaching* 20.40 (2019): 35–36.

Shasha, Tamsin, Lucy Ruddiman, and Mark Katz. Personal interview. 27 Apr. 2023.

Taylor, Diana. *The Archive and the Repertoire: Performing Cultural Memory in the Americas*. Duke University Press, 2003.

4 The King's Greek Play and the Classics Ecology

Peter Swallow

All theatre is a dialogue between the different people who come together to produce and receive it. The King's Greek Play, an annual performance of a play in Greek by university students at King's College London, is no less made up of generations of interactions between students and staff, audience and performers. Its audiences have always been largely formed of schoolchildren studying the ancient world while its cast and crew have predominantly come from the KCL student body (mostly Classics students) with varying degrees of departmental intervention. So the Greek Play has an important role in shaping the wider UK Classics ecology, to some extent from the bottom up—that is, at the school and undergraduate levels.[1]

This chapter makes extensive use of the King's Greek Play's archive, housed in the Classics Department at KCL, to set out how the interactions between the various actors who have contributed to the institution of the Play embed it within the UK Classics ecology, and how that ecology has functioned reciprocally to shape the development of the Play as an institution. As with any institution, the Greek Play has changed slowly, accompanied by lapses of institutional memory. But the understanding of what sorts of knowledge and value can be drawn out from the texts being performed is now very different from when the King's Greek Play was first staged, and as the interests of the UK Classics ecology have shifted over time, so has the position of the Play within that ecology.

The King's Greek Play in the Classics Ecology

The tradition of staging plays in ancient Greek at British universities goes back to 1880, when Oxford students staged *Agamemnon* (Hall and Macintosh, 452–454). KCL's annual tradition of a Greek Play started in 1953. Although the idea for it came from the students, not the Department, it was nevertheless strongly inspired by the arrival of Professor R. P. Winnington-Ingram to the College. His lectures on Greek tragedy gripped the undergraduate body, and as two of his students explained, 'a fever for Greek drama took hold of us, and we soon formed the idea that we would 'put on a play'—in the original Greek ... Winnington-Ingram was interested, but wary' (Sparkes and Sparkes). Another impetus was the Cambridge Greek Play—as one student explained, she had 'sent off for tickets to the [G]reek [P]lay at Cambridge. However, we were too late to obtain them, so I proposed: "Why don't we produce our own play?"'[2] This first performance—Euripides' *Hippolytus*— was put on by the student-run Classical Society, an internal student society designed for Classics students to both socialise and explore their interests in Classics beyond the university curriculum. Ultimately, 'few saw the production' and Winnington-Ingram's response to it was characteristically brusque (Sparkes and Sparkes). He told the Classical Society that 'it would be worth bringing in an expert for elementary lessons in simple attitudes and gestures'[3]—or, to put it another way, they needed to learn how to act. Remembering the play 50 years later, one actor would recall: 'I don't think it entered our heads to seek the help of the academic staff.... We were not sure that we had them on our side'.[4]

Nevertheless, *Hippolytus* received a glowing review in *The Times*, which hoped that 'this society will succeed in establishing a tradition of Greek plays in London' ('"Hippolytus" in Greek'). The positivity of the review was no doubt helped by the fact that it was written by a member of the faculty, though published anonymously.[5] Despite the smallness of the production and its inadequacies as a piece of theatre, then, from the very beginning there was an understanding that the King's Greek Play could play an important role within the wider Classics ecology in establishing a regular point of contact between universities and those beyond the academy. For this reason if for no other, it was worthy of receiving national press attention, facilitated by the intervention of an academic from the department, which included a call for the exchange of knowledge offered by the Greek Play to continue on as a tradition. This was despite the students' uncertainty about the faculty's support.

From its inception, the King's Greek Play has been a major part of Classics at KCL, particularly among students. Not just actors, but directors, producers, designers, make-up artists, ushers, business managers, publicity managers— the village of people involved in any amateur production—have always been drawn from the student body. For many, there was a strong expectation that Classics students at KCL needed to *do their part* for the King's Play—which at times appeared more as a duty than reward. At a special meeting of the Classical Society to discuss the Greek Play in 1975, one member

> asked whether the Play was really necessary and Miss Norbron explained that it was, due to "tradition" ... Miss Haynes felt that if the Play were even more dragged out than at present, members would only get more fed up ... Mr. Durrant claimed it should be enjoyed, but Miss Russell said that some people had a fear of the Play, which they could not avoid.[6]

44 *Peter Swallow*

As they were so integral to the production of the play, KCL's student body could shape its direction in very concrete ways. In 1959, Euripides' *Heracles* was performed, and the choice of a play with a male chorus was mandated by the small number of women undergraduates available that year.[7] For a time through the 1990s, academic credit was also given for participation in the play so that very active members could be moved up a degree band if they had just missed out because of their commitment.[8] Copies of the (rather robust) grading sheets for individual members of the cast and crew survive in the archive.[9] This formalisation of the Greek Play should be seen as an acknowledgement of its institutional weight, even if, in practice, it remained a largely student-led undertaking.

Although it is certainly still an institution delivered and underpinned by Classics students, any expectation of participation has shifted. The Classics Department at KCL has become significantly larger than it was in 1953, when only a handful of students would join in a given year, and most students do not take part in the production. If the Play has become less central to KCL Classics, however, it is nevertheless still an important part of the wider UK Classics ecology in several ways.

For one, the Play has consistently attracted a large audience. A summary of attendance figures from 1964 to 1991 (Table 4.1) indicates that the average performance was seen by over 1,000 people (excluding two cancelled productions in 1979 and 1986).[10] This indicates a healthy appetite for academically

Table 4.1 Summary of audience numbers for King's Greek Play, 1964–1991[11]

Year	Attendance
1964	c. 725
1965	c. 774
1966	c. 725
1968	c. 900?
1974	'A very bad year (but no records)'
1976	c. 1,522
1977	c. 1,461
1978	c. 1,523
1980	879
1983	883
1984	1,552
1985	1,492
1986	**487 (booked: 1136)**
1987	1,129
1988	1,670
1989	790
1990	1,334
1991	1,618

Bold indicates a cancelled production.

situated performances of Greek drama, particularly in London where so many school students who study classical subjects reside (Hunt and Holmes-Henderson). It is also a marker of the Greek Play's enduring legacy and reputation, of course.

More important than raw numbers, however, the real value of the Greek Play has always been as outreach to schools—and this has been the case since long before the academy started to talk about outreach as an important aspect of a university's societal role. It is difficult to say how many audience-members annually are schoolchildren, or what percentage of those attendees come from state-maintained schools, but it was presumed in 1989 that 'the majority of the audience comes from the independent sector'.[12] Nor is it possible to say how many who have attended knew Greek. The archive suggests non-Greek students *did* attend; in 1988, teacher Marion Baldock 'took a group of 22 'A' level classical civilisation students to the play... none of them knew any ancient Greek. They thoroughly enjoyed the performance'.[13] Certainly, the growth of classical civilisation over Greek as a school subject over the course of the King's Greek Play's history must mean that in recent years, many audience members do not study Greek. In 2022, 3,457 students took classical civilisation GCSE and 2,959 took the A Level, compared with only 982 GCSE Greek students and 206 A Level students ('Key Stage 4 Performance').

The King's Greek Play sits alongside other major performances of Greek drama staged at other universities, the most important and best established of which are the UCL, Cambridge and Oxford Greek Plays. UCL's play is performed in English, while Oxford and Cambridge stage their plays triennially. This has meant that the different productions have always attracted slightly different audiences. Nevertheless, all four established Greek Plays—all performed in south-east England—are marketed towards schools, and have schoolchildren make up a significant part of their audience.

The interaction between these different play institutions within the Classics ecology is hard to define, but important. As already noted, it was the success of Cambridge's and Oxford's Greek Plays that inspired KCL (and UCL) to set up their own.[14] For several years after 1988, UCL and KCL both took part in the London Festival of Greek Drama, an attempt to raise the profile of both productions. A couple of insights from the archive give the sense to which these two Plays have interacted within the wider UK Classics ecology—not always harmoniously. In 1990, members of the KCL Classical Society attended UCL's production of *Antigone* and wrote a catty review of the production in the Society scrap-book—highlighting in particular the UCL students' inability to act.[15] And in 1995, Michael Silk, a lecturer at KCL intimately involved in the production of the King's Play, wrote to his counterpart Gerald O'Daly at UCL to try to stop the two performances from clashing, and therefore cannibalising each other's audience numbers: 'I was appalled to learn just now that your students are proposing, unilaterally, to change dates for your play to the same week as ours ... is there anything (else) that can be done?'[16] Among both students and faculty, then, there has long been a certain tension between the two institutions and an understanding that they compete uncomfortably for space within the wider UK Classics ecology.

Students and staff may both have been invested in the success of the King's Play, but they have consistently had different motivations for their involvement, affected by their perception of the Play's function. For the faculty, there has always been a sense of the kudos attained by harbouring such an institution as the King's Greek Play—which is why both the play and its archive feature prominently on the Classics Department's website ('The Greek Play'). There is also the acknowledgement that outreach and impact are now major parts of a university department's social function, as assessed by the current Research Excellence Framework for example, and that the Greek Play may be used as a recruitment tool for new undergraduates. Meanwhile, for students, the focus has tended to be on the actual production of the play itself, as well as all the accompanying social aspects—the minutes of a Classical Society meeting in 1955 indicate a key issue was who was to pay for the cast party.[17] I do not mean to suggest that the faculty are incapable of considering the social or aesthetic purposes of the play, or that students fail to grasp the importance of academic outreach. But it is certainly true that the department staff have been more concerned with how the Greek Play interacts with the UK Classics ecology and affects KCL's standing within that ecology, than students.

The tension between these two important actors in the Play's production—students and faculty—has existed consistently since the play's founding. This came to a head in 1986 with a particularly disastrous production of *Bacchae*. The director, Robert Peacock, also cast himself as Dionysus and the entire production was under-rehearsed—by opening night, nobody knew their lines. Ultimately, 'owing to a series of misfortunes, culminating in the illness of [Peacock], the last four performances had to be cancelled'.[18] This led to a series of inquisitions being carried out by the Department to find out what had happened, and in the wake of a very public embarrassment—having to cancel a play that dozens of schools, as well as alumni, had arranged to see—it was decided that the institution was too important to remain in the hands of the student society any longer. Going forward, the Greek Play would be run by a student-staff committee, and a member of staff would be appointed Executive Producer. Michael Silk was the first to take up this role. In his advertisement for the 1987 production team, Silk suggested a Latin play be chosen;[19] in the end, no such break in tradition materialised. Robert Peacock, however, was able to make his return to the Play, being cast as Agamemnon in Sophocles' *Ajax*—this decision presumably motivated either by a spirit of clemency, or perhaps more likely, a realistic acknowledgement that the world of the King's Play was too small to allow for the bearing of grudges.

Michael Silk's long and deep involvement with the King's Greek Play had begun slightly earlier in 1977, when for a production of Aristophanes' *Clouds* he arranged a jazz score including well-known tunes such as 'Somewhere Over the Rainbow' to create an incongruous puzzle of recognition highly appropriate to the word games inherent to Aristophanic comedy.[20] For 1981's production of Aristophanes' *Wasps*, Silk again wrote a jazz score setting some of the choral elements to well-known songs (Neville). This was also the first of a series of plays to be taken on an ambitious tour of American universities, a project organised and led by Silk.[21] Silk's heavy involvement in the Greek Play over many years was therefore facilitated not only by his philological expertise—although this was certainly a factor—but also his musical ability, organisational skills, willingness to be involved and, as he became synonymous with the Play, a deep institutional memory.

For the second North American Tour in 1983, Silk took on the role of director and adaptor as well as organiser. These tours demonstrate the importance of the King's Greek Play to the institution of Classics at KCL, and reflect an attempt to widen the scope of its engagement beyond London and the Southeast of England. But their success can be questioned. In 1988, 'a party of fifteen, including eleven performers, took a quite elaborate production of Aristophanes' most complex comedy [the *Frogs*] to a record number of universities on both coasts of the USA…. Well over 2,000 people saw us perform'.[22] Despite Silk's positive tone, however, this is not a substantial audience for a three-week, international tour with 17 performances—an average of just over 100 audience-members per performance.[23] Moreover, the ambitious nature of these tours did not necessarily support the King's Play performances back in London. In fact, 'the 1988 KCL Greek Play Tour was in financial difficulties and had applied to KCCP [the King's College Classics Play committee] for a grant of £1000'.[24] An attempt to tour in 1990 was abandoned because of insufficient ticket sales. And, after Michael Silk stepped back from heavy involvement in the Play, a breakdown between the staff and students put the 1994 touring production of *Agamemnon* in jeopardy. Staff-member Hugh Bowden took over the organisation from Silk, but the student Business Manager, Alex Taylor, resigned, leaving (another staff-member) Michael Trapp to step in. Bowden wrote to Silk expressing the 'enormous strain' he was under and seeking to be relieved of the role.[25] The tours could not, therefore, live up to their aspirations, and were not logistically possible without the heavy involvement of Silk.

More recently, the importance of the King's Greek Play has been reflected in the appointment of an experienced executive producer to oversee the production's artistic output. David Bullen, one of the editors of this volume, fulfilled this role from 2015 to 2021. Bullen is an academic, but also a theatre practitioner who co-founded By Jove Theatre Company in 2011. In 2023, the Greek Play was 'overseen' by Actors of Dionysus, another professional theatre company specialising in Greek drama ('The Greek Play').[26] This investment in the Greek Play—both financially and artistically—speaks to the growing importance of the Play to the Department, as well as to changes in the Classics ecology, such as increased collaboration between theatre makers and academics (see Plastow, this volume).

The Greekness of the Greek Play

Whenever something becomes a 'tradition', it can be hard to interrogate it, and ask what justifies its status as an institution. Plays performed in ancient Greek immediately put up a barrier to easy accessibility, because they use a performance language which none of the audience and actors speak fluently. Yet for many, that barrier is part of their value. Performance in general is not as ephemeral as it first appears but is instead 'an important system of knowing and transmitting knowledge' (Taylor, 26; see also Bullen, this volume). In a broad sense, performance always speaks to a wider network of knowledge and ideas—an interaction which will live beyond the specific moment of performance in the memories of the performers and audience, in institutional memory, and of course in the archive.

Tradition has always been important for the King's Greek Play, which is why, even in the first review of the first play back in 1953, the reviewer hoped that KCL 'will succeed in establishing a tradition of Greek plays in London' ('"Hippolytus" in Greek'). But the Play has also invited innovation, particularly in its recent history. The ways in which tradition and innovation have interacted within the institution of the Play speak to the shifts in the UK Classics ecology more widely. Broadly speaking, as our discipline has increasingly valued knowledge beyond that of Greek philology, so has the King's Greek Play found new idioms in which to express itself beyond accurate recitation; as the Classics ecology has become more diverse in terms of educational background as well as what is valued, so has the King's Greek Play attempted to speak to other kinds of value which can be drawn from ancient theatre.

For the first years of the Greek Play the foremost focus of the production was an accurate recitation of the Greek. This was to achieve a sense of 'authenticity',[27] albeit authenticity of a very narrow, philological sort. Acting ability was secondary at best—despite Winnington-Ingram's advice to the contrary. Lesley Boatwright, who played Chrysothemis in the 1956 production of Sophocles' *Electra*, provided a first-hand account of this philological focus:

> To act in front of an audience that sits following the words of one's speech in printed texts is shattering ... I missed a line out of my speech; two schoolboys in the front row looked at each other. "She's missed a line out!" announced one, in a penetrating whisper. The chorus leader, sitting at the edge of the stage, glared them into silence. I clutched my basket of burnt offerings, and started the stichomythia too soon.[28]

Her fear is not provoked by the stress of performing but of properly delivering the lines, and it is deficiencies in her memory of the Greek that she and her audience react to. Indeed, the expectation that lines should be delivered accurately is one shared by both performer and audience.

The difficulty of balancing accurate recitation with effective dramatisation was reflected in reviews. The *Times* reviewer noted of the 1957 *Orestes* that while 'the undergraduate company … speak their lines with absolute clearness', 'they do not cover much emotional range' ('King's College, London: The "Orestes" of Euripides'). In 1959, when *Heracles* was performed, the reviewer noted that 'the verse was excellently articulated throughout … but nearly the whole company accepted with excessive equanimity the horrors they witnessed and the agony of the lines they spoke or heard' ('Hercules Furens: Riddle of a Play by Euripides'). In 1960, the Classical Society took the bold decision to stage the newly discovered Menander play, *Dyskolos*.[29] This was their first comedy, though this time the reviewer criticised them for failing to recite accurately. Apparently, they all 'spoke too hurriedly and many lines were lost' ('The Dyskolos in Greek: London Students' Production').

The first King's Greek Play which appears to have experimented with 'lapses into English' was Aristophanes' *Birds* in 1982 (Teague; note the reviewer's loaded term!). Euripides' *Heracles* was produced in 1983 with the notable addition of an English prologue (Ruscoe). But for the second North American Tour in 1983, an even bolder experiment was attempted. Silk, as director, combined elements of *Heracles*, *Alcestis*, and *Frogs* with a new English script to produce, in his words, 'an interaction between the two languages and, more fundamentally, an immediacy of theatrical effect without prejudice to the power and authenticity of the Greek texts'.[30] Audiences responded warmly to this model, although ironically 'the biggest target for criticism … was that much of the play remained in Greek.'[31]

This innovation did not carry across into the domestic production. In 1984, to mark the thirtieth anniversary of the Greek Play, King's revived Euripides' *Hippolytus* in an 'unadventurous' traditional performance idiom, all in Greek (Coleman). Again, this decision can be linked back to the sense of tradition— as the production was consciously echoing the first performance of *Hippolytus* in 1953, it was perhaps felt that it needed to be as traditional as possible. Alumni have always had a powerful influence on the Greek Play.[32] Subsequent productions did not experiment with English much further. It took until 2003 for the Greek Play to even be surtitled in English (Mercer).

This initial and lasting focus on the Greek text was of course shaped by the Greek Play's location in a university Classics department, and heavily influenced by the older institutions of the Cambridge and Oxford Greek Plays— both performed in the original language. Michael Silk explained to me that there was 'a sense of decorum' underlying the play, a sense that 'it's appropriate for a Classics department which teaches Classical languages' to stage its dramas in the original language.[33] This was not without an appreciation of the limitations of performing in Greek—as Winnington-Ingram himself had obviously seen in 1953. A disgruntled audience-member wrote to the President of the Classical Society in 1966 after coming to see Euripides' *Iphigenia in Tauris* to say that 'the obvious, and understandable, limitations of the actors should have made the presentation of the English version more reasonable. However, I must assume that tradition had to prevail'.[34] As Taylor has reflected, 'performances may not … give us access and insight into another culture, but they certainly tell us a great deal about our desire for access, and reflect the politics of our interpretations' (Taylor, 6). The original decision to stage the play in Greek, as well as the ongoing decision to continue to do so every year, reflects the Play's politics of accessibility. With the focus being on the language of the play, it was most obviously accessible, first and foremost, to students of ancient Greek.

Perhaps justifiable in 1953. But today, far more school students learning about the ancient world access it in English than in Greek. In June 2019, at time of writing the last year of good data because of the pandemic, 3612 students took classical civilisation GCSE and 2964 the A-Level; compare that to 1161 GCSE Greek students and only 215 Greek A-Level takers. Meanwhile, 85% of those GCSE Greek students were at independent schools—72% of GCSE classical civilisation students were (Holmes-Henderson et al.). Maybe there is still pedagogic benefit to exposing students not learning Greek to the sounds of the language—perhaps for some it might inspire them to learn Greek, for instance. But as a tool of educational outreach, it is surely not the way to make ancient drama feel as accessible as possible to the largest majority of Classics students from the broadest range of backgrounds. Of course, even A-Level Greek students cannot be expected to truly understand spoken Greek. To focus on Greek students, then, is to focus on a far too narrow band of potential attendees.

In recent years, an understanding of the changing nature of Classics in the UK has caused a sea-change in the approach taken to the Greekness of the Greek Play. The plays selected now track those which appear on the classical civilisation A-Level and GCSE specifications (not necessarily the Greek specs), a reflection of the ongoing pedagogical importance of the Greek Play. Because of this change, for 2018's production of Euripides' *Medea* and 2019's of Sophocles' *Antigone*, Executive Producer David Bullen decided to blend Greek and English. This was not as radical a departure as it seemed at the time—as has been seen, the Greek Play had long experimented with different ways to introduce English elements to the play even if institutional memory has failed to recall this. University Classics departments are as likely to reinvent previously attempted methods of outreach as they are to forget what has already worked.

There is another reason why the Greek Play is no longer entirely in Greek. In 1998, King's performed Sophocles' *Oedipus the King*, and for the first time there is clear archival evidence that an actor did not know their Greek. One audience-member, whose views were captured by survey after the play, remarked that 'Oedipus didn't know what he was saying and to the last responded with the wrong lines! The dialogue was consistently gobbledy-gook, making no sense at all.'[35] Just as the wider UK Classics ecology has changed, so too has Classics at KCL. The Classics Department is much larger than in 1953, but the number of students arriving with a good grasp of Greek already is now very small indeed. Like at all universities (including Oxford and Cambridge), the undergraduate degree is no longer as philologically focussed (some might say, philologically *rigorous*)—students now spend more of their time thinking about the social history of the ancient world, or its reception, or its material culture, and less drilling its languages. Most classicists pick up Greek as first- or second-year undergraduates, if at all. Moreover, as the department has grown bigger, it has also become more disparate. Fewer Classics students want to take part in the play—or feel pressure to do so—and conversely there is more interest from talented, Greek-less performers in other departments. So the standard of Greek, so well praised in the reviews of early plays, has understandably diminished, and it is increasingly common for performers like 1998's Oedipus to simply make up some Greek-sounding 'gobbledy-gook'. As the term 'classicist' has begun to encompass a wider range of skills and types of people, the world of KCL Classics has changed with it. The King's Greek Play has, eventually, shifted in response.

The Future of the King's Greek Play

An even more radical departure took place in 2020, based not only on the legacy of the Greek Play but also on a more recent King's tradition—its reputation as a leading centre for classical reception. *Dionysus in the Underworld* was an entirely new play weaving together Euripides' *Bacchae* and Aristophanes' *Frogs*, with Greek text taken from both plays alongside English translation and new writing. Importantly, it was produced 'in collaboration with current students'—a return to the Greek Play's origins and a shift in creative power (Department of Classics at King's College London).

Due to the pandemic, a performance based on fragmentary Greek tragedy and the Trojan war cycle was given online in 2021—an opportunity seized upon to drive the Greek Play as far as possible from tradition. For the only time in the Play's history, the production was entirely in English. The play was written by students, but Bullen and professional theatre designer Nicola Hewitt-George, who collaborated on the project, worked with the students to understand how to write a script and tell stories effectively.

The Greek Play returned fully in 2022 with 'The Plague at Thebes', which offered 'a contemporary response to Sophocles' [Theban] plays', again with Greek and English elements ('The Greek Play'). A reduced production of *Oedipus the King* was performed in Greek within a framing narrative of *Antigone*, rewritten and reimagined in a new English text. This blended approach allowed the play to speak more directly to contemporary political issues. The

2020 *Dionysus* examined climate change; the 2022 *Plague at Thebes* explored 'the social and political consequences of an unprecedented pandemic, civil disobedience, and the place and responsibility of an individual within society' ('The Greek Play'). This new direction can be understood as a response to a wider Classics ecology increasingly concerned with how it interacts with the world beyond Classics to discuss important issues of social justice.

The more radical political statement of this new format, however, is the overhaul of a 70-year-old institution. Meanwhile, the continued presence of Greek text speaks to the importance of tradition, hopefully in a more accessible form for the twenty-first century. The King's Greek Play has re-centred itself in the twenty-first-century Classics ecology, and reasserted its important role as a pedagogical institution within that ecology, even as the Classics ecology has acted to shape the Play. Tradition is a fine thing, but so too is bold innovation when used for the celebration and promotion of Classics both within, and beyond, the academy.

Notes

1. I am myself an alumnus of the King's Greek Play—in 2018, I played Creon in Euripides' *Medea*.
2. Letter from Theresa G. Ferrar to Frieda Klotz, 27 May 2007, King's Greek Play Archive, uncatalogued.
3. 'Tuesday. Dec. 15th', Classical Society Minute Book, KCL Department of Classics.
4. Brian Sparkes, *Hippolytus* Programme, King's Greek Play Archive, 03008.
5. Letter from Theresa G. Ferrar to Professor Schiesaro, 1 February 2000, King's Greek Play Archive, uncatalogued.
6. Budget Reports 1953–1974, King's Greek Play Archive, uncatalogued.
7. 'Meeting on October 7th 1958', Classical Society Minute Book, KCL Department of Classics.
8. In the UK, undergraduate degrees can be awarded with First Class, Upper-Second Class (2:1), Lower-Second Class (2:2) or Third Class Honours.
9. For example, for the 1991 production of Sophocles' *Oedipus the King*, students were graded on scope of contribution; effort; and quality, from A to D. This was then converted into credits. The director, J. Leigh-Hunt, was awarded an A for scope and effort—but only a CB for quality. Oedipus, meanwhile (played by A. Walsh-Taylor) was given a more positive A–A–AAB. Michael Silk appears to have graded the students, with sign-off from the head of department. King's Greek Play Archive, 91018.
10. The 1979 production was cancelled because 'rehearsals did not go according to [the producer's] plan, partly because (it was said) some members of the cast found it difficult to attend' (Letter from John [unreadable] to Brian and Diana Sparkes, 11 January 2003, King's Greek Play Archive, uncatalogued). The 1986 production is discussed later in this chapter (46).
11. Summary of audience figures and profits, King's Greek Play Archive, gen010. Not all years are recorded. The figures are sometimes worked out based on income from ticket sales so should be taken as illustrative not definitive.
12. Letter from Andrew Stevenson to Michael Silk, 10 July 1986, King's Greek Play Archive, uncatalogued.

13 'Aristophanes' Frogs, King's College London, Department of Classics, 16-19 March 1988' [Review], Marion Baldock, King's Greek Play Archive, uncatalogued.
14 It is unsurprising that the four most well-known university Greek plays all take place in London and the South East, considering the distribution of schools teaching classical subjects (Hunt and Holmes Henderson; see Plastow and Bullen, this volume, p. 5). Bradfield College, a school just outside of Reading (so also in the South East), also performs a well-established triennial Greek Play.
15 *Classical Society Scrap-Book*, 1990, King's Greek Play Archive, uncatalogued.
16 Letter from Michael Silk to Gerard O'Daly, 9 November 1995, King's Greek Play Archive, 96010.
17 *Classical Society Minute Book*, 22 February 1955, King's Greek Play Archive, uncatalogued.
18 Letter from Michael Silk, 19 March 1986, King's Greek Play Archive, 86005.
19 Note from Michael Silk ('Producer designate'), King's Greek Play Archive, 86010.
20 Interview with Michael Silk, 4 April 2022. For more on Silk's innovative use of music in the Greek Play, see Silk.
21 Tours took place in 1981, 1983, 1985, 1988 and 1994.
22 The *Frogs* Tour of America, 1988 [Report by Michael Silk], King's Greek Play Archive, 88027.
23 The *Frogs* Tour of America, 1988 [Report by Michael Silk], King's Greek Play Archive, 88027.
24 Business Manager's Cash Book (1975–1990), King's Greek Play Archive, uncatalogued.
25 Letter from Hugh Bowden to Michael Silk, 14 February 1994, King's Greek Play Archive, 94006.
26 This chapter was written before the 2023 Play was staged.
27 Gamel, 155: 'Classical scholars, relying on their knowledge of the scripts and their ideas about the impact of the original productions, often idealise, explicitly or implicitly, the "original form" of ancient drama, and find contemporary productions wanting.'
28 Lesley Boatwright, 'Ordeal by Acting' [personal account], King's Greek Play Archive, 56004.
29 This play had been first published in 1958–1959, 'the most important event [of the year] for the classical scholar' (Goold, 139). It was performed several times in 1959 and 1960. The University of Sydney staged a performance in Greek in 1959 (APGRD 4838).
30 Michael Silk, King's Greek Play Tour 1983: Report, King's Greek Play Archive, uncatalogued.
31 Michael Silk, King's Greek Play Tour 1983: Report, King's Greek Play Archive, uncatalogued.
32 When *Hippolytus* was performed in 2003 to mark 50 years of the Greek Play, the original Hippolytus, Brian A. Sparkes, was even invited to write a programme note on the original performance (Brian Sparkes, *Hippolytus* Programme, King's Greek Play Archive, 03008). A reunion was held for previous Greek Play performers ('Golden Jubilee for Greek Play').
33 Interview with Michael Silk, 4 April 2022.
34 [Unknown] to 'The President, The Classical Society', 8 March 1966. King's Greek Play Archive no. 66005.
35 Audience Response, King's Greek Play Archive, 98011. Of course, unless the audience-member's own Greek was very good, they must have been following along with a crib—how else could they tell accurate Greek from 'gobbledy-gook' themselves?

Works Cited

Coleman, Danielle. 'King's College Greek Play.' *LACT Newsletter* 35 (1984): 15.
Department of Classics at King's College London. 'Dionysus in the Underworld.' *Facebook*, 14 January 2020, https://www.facebook.com/kingsclassics/photos/pb.187047304670735.-2207520000./3385584834816950/?type=3&eid=ARAMMAbiLHaJtHFcp920gtldoCPZTOmvtARunxcrOBmKaB1waGO5MSPtNlOMoeBDTaJCg3BjyQRLjdTl. Accessed 18 Aug. 2022.
Gamel, Mary-Kay. 'Revising 'Authenticity' in Staging Ancient Mediterranean Drama.' *Theorising Performance*, edited by Edith Hall and Stephe Harrop, Bristol Classical Press, 2010, 153–170.
'Golden Jubilee for Greek Play.' *The Comment* 145 (February 2003): 16.
Goold, G.P. 'First Thoughts on the *Dyscolus*.' *Phoenix* 13.4 (1959): 139–160.
Hall, Edith, and Fiona Macintosh. *Greek Tragedy and the British Theatre 1660–1914*. Oxford University Press, 2005.
'Hercules Furens: Riddle of a Play by Euripides.' *The Times*, 5 March 1959, 3.
'"Hippolytus" in Greek.' *The Times*, 28 November 1953, 8.
Liverpool Classical Press, forthcoming.
Hunt, Steven, and Arlene Holmes-Henderson. 'A Level Classics Poverty: Classical Subjects in Schools in England: Access, Attainment and Progression.' *Council of University Classical Departments Bulletin* 50 (2021): 1–26.
'Key Stage 4 Performance.' Department for Education, 2022. https://explore-education-statistics.service.gov.uk/find-statistics/key-stage-4-performance-revised/2021-22. Accessed 21 Mar. 2023
'King's College, London: The "Orestes" of Euripides.' *The Times*, 22 February 1957, 3.
Mercer, Cathy. 'Review of King's College Greek Play.' *LACT Newsletter* 72 (2003): 5f.
Neville, J. 'Aristophanes: Wasps.' *LACT Newsletter* 29 (1981): 9.
'Results Statistics.' OCR, 2023. https://www.ocr.org.uk/administration/results-statistics/. Accessed 21 Mar. 2023.
Ruscoe, Jo. 'King's College Play: The Heracles of Euripides.' *LACT Newsletter* 33 (1983): 11.
Silk, Michael. 'Translating/Transposing Aristophanes.' *Aristophanes in Performance*, edited by Edith Hall and Amanda Wrigley, Legenda, 2007, 287–308.
Sparkes, Diana, and Brian Sparkes. 'Obituary: Professor R. P. Winnington-Ingram.' *The Independent*, 5 February 1993. https://www.independent.co.uk/news/people/obituary-professor-r-p-winningtoningram-1471003.html. Accessed 18 Aug. 2023.
Taylor, Diana. *The Archive and the Repertoire*. Duke University Press, 2003.
Teague, M. 'Aristophanes' "Birds" at King's College.' *LACT Newsletter* 31 (1982): 12.
'The Dyskolos in Greek: London Students' Production.' *The Times*, 11 March 1960, 15.
'The Greek Play.' KCL Department of Classics, undated. https://www.kcl.ac.uk/classics/about/greekplay. Accessed 22 June 2022.

Part II
Choral Practice and Participation

5 Greek Tragedy in the Drama Studio
Lecoq, Agonism, and the Politics of Choral Pedagogy

Stephe Harrop

The drama studio is a place of contradictions. Like the twentieth-century actor-training systems it came into being alongside, the studio is an environment designed 'to harness the actor's creativity, inspiration, and talent through the introduction of disciplined techniques' (Hodge xiii). It is a place for consolidating and extending the creative capacities of performers-in-training, both as individuals and as collectives. But it is also a location where (as Ali Hodge indicates) personal expressivity encounters 'discipline' and 'technique'; a place where emerging theatre-artists' energies may be 'harnessed' towards particular cultural, social, and political ends. In consequence, the drama studio represents an important (and under-explored) site for reflecting on formations and flows of knowledge and understanding in relation to ancient Greek tragedy.

The antecedents of today's drama studios were energised by utopian ideals and ambitions. As Tom Cornford has observed, in its earliest form the studio was a 'small, experimental theatre' (4), incorporating 'elements of both theatre and school' (5). The emergence of these spaces in the early twentieth century signalled aspirations towards the cultivation of long-term collaborative practices aimed at new ways of making theatrical art:

> [...] their approach to making theatre emphasised the creativity of the actor, the crucial function of collective training for the process of theatre-making, and the importance of experimentation with alternative styles and traditions in order to reinvigorate the contemporary theatre. (8)

Such desires were never without wider cultural and political resonance, including a 'commitment to collaboration' and to 'continually revising their work' which indicated 'at least theoretical concessions to more egalitarian and democratic approaches' (8). Since such organisations generated 'models of practice that would shape the curricula of drama schools' (300), the black-box drama studios of contemporary UK higher education, where students in performing arts undertake a large portion of their practical learning, owe at least some of their identity to the idealistic energies of a century ago.

DOI: 10.4324/b22844-7

Yet, despite these lofty ideals, the drama studio today is also a site permeated with prejudice, inequity, and legacies of harm. In 2016, Maame Atuah, Mumba Dodwell, and Steven Kavuma founded The Diversity School, a grassroots organisation committed to addressing 'under-representation, access and diversity in UK drama schools' (Rogers 2). Five years later, The Diversity School's final report testifies to ongoing and damaging discrimination on the basis of race, gender, social class, and disability (Rogers). The impact of the #MeToo movement has revealed that, for many students, the drama studio has been a place where—under the guise of creative freedom and industry preparation—abuses have been perpetrated with near-impunity (Cavendish & Goldsbrough; Cavendish; Yossman). Too often, the drama studio has been a place where talented young people have been taught to abdicate their own judgment and safety, placing themselves at risk to gain the approval of powerful elders. Actor and writer Michaela Coel, whose memoir *Misfits* documents the fact that her London drama school would only permit a black student to star in a classical drama (*Lysistrata*) in a low-prestige venue on the wrong side of the river (2021, 47–48),[1] describes a training culture which actively perpetuated disempowering and harmful tropes: 'We were told at school, if we wanted to pursue this, we should be "yes" people, and expect to be poor for the rest of our lives.' (44).[2]

Inevitably, students' encounters with Greek tragedy within such educational institutions are shaped by a swirl of ideological cross-currents, no less powerful for being largely submerged. Advocating an 'insider approach to practice-based pedagogical arts research' (537), Jamieson Dryburgh proposes that 'the studio can be considered as a situated cultural site', a 'location wherein shared and learned patterns of values, behaviour, beliefs and language of a culture-sharing group become established' (541). Accordingly, this chapter considers the ways in which Classics education takes place within the drama studio; the understandings of ancient theatre practice and its current meanings which are (explicitly or tacitly) promulgated within studio settings; and the implications of dominant training models and practices for wider cultural understandings and imaginings of Greek tragedy in the UK today. It contends that in failing to recognise or acknowledge the (culturally conservative) ideological underpinnings of established approaches, the customary pedagogies of UK HE are often unable to confront students with a Greek tragedy capable of intersecting meaningfully with their own lived experiences of power, dissent, struggle, and aspiration. The discussion developed here specifically focuses on approaches to choral training derived from Jacques Lecoq's theatre pedagogy, critically analysing dominant practices currently in use in UK drama studios and tracing the emergence of an alternative approach to Lecoq-inspired choral training, aimed at empowering students as creative agents, both within and beyond the studio.

Jacques Lecoq is an important figure in studio-based receptions of Greek tragedy in the UK. Exercises and approaches developed at his

École internationale de théâtre in Paris (founded 1956), and then disseminated through English-speaking education systems following the publication of David Bradby's translation of *The Moving Body (Le Corps Poétique)* in 2000,[3] have become foundational elements of drama, theatre, and acting curricula nationwide, including in drama school (conservatoire) and university settings. Perhaps the single most recognisable pedagogic device in today's studio-based chorus work derives from a practice briefly outlined in *The Moving Body*:

> Another type of exercise is when a chorus moves without anyone knowing who is the leader. The internal rule, which spectators are unaware of, but the students discover, is that the leader is inevitably the one visible to all the others. (140)

In Lecoq's discussion, this is one of several potential approaches outlined, all of them aiming at achieving a sense of the tragic chorus as 'a kind of living cell, capable of taking on different forms according to the situation in which it finds itself' (139). He also, for example, presents exercises which involve reenacting political speeches from history (138), or improvising group reactions to 'a football match, a film, a bullfight' (138–139). But, despite Lecoq's own experimental variety of approaches, it is the briefly sketched exercise invoking a chorus with no visible leader which has been most eagerly adopted in UK drama studios.

In the course of this adoption, the favoured exercise has been both removed from its experimental pedagogic context and progressively miniaturised. In her study of Lecoq's choruses, Shona Morris draws attention to the fact that participants in such training may choose the 'metaphor' which defines their chorus's presence at each moment of a tragic narrative, giving as examples: 'a group of animals (a shoal of fish or a flock of birds), elements (a wave or a cloud), matter that changes (glass shatters, paper crumbles, mercury roils)' (152). However, where Morris' discussion foregrounds participants' capacity and responsibility to make successive creative choices about the nature of their emerging chorus, Helen Eastman's survey of UK receptions of Lecoq's work demonstrates how a single, reduced version of this practice has largely become canonical, citing: 'a group who can move as one body, like a flock of birds or shoal of fish' (364).

The widespread adoption of this specific exercise was informed by the work of UK theatre company Complicité, whose founder members met while studying at Lecoq's school, and whose artistic director (Simon McBurney) has played a major role in shaping UK receptions of Lecoq's ensemble practices (Eastman 363). In particular, their 1992 production *The Street of Crocodiles* showcased ensemble dramaturgies in which actors aimed to emulate the in-flight motion of a flock of starlings (Giannachi & Luckhurst 74; Heddon & Milling 178–179), an approach which gained significant cultural reach when the company's rehearsals were documented for television in an episode of *The Late Show* (BBC, 1992). Within a few years, modified versions of the Lecoq exercise, filtered through Complicité manifestations, began to appear in guides to physical theatre training. For instance, Dymphna Callery's 2001 *Through the Body* gives an iteration titled 'Shoal of fish' (94), with a preamble expressly name-checking *The Street of Crocodiles* as inspiration (94). Two decades on, versions of this same exercise have become ubiquitous enough that they circulate without reference to (any of) its originators. In an educational resource prepared by Actors of Dionysus it is simply called the 'Diamond Exercise for Chorus Work', though a note for teachers explaining that students 'should look like a shoal of fish, or birds flocking' makes the debt clear.[4] It is also notable, by this point, that the exploratory range of potential approaches documented in *The Moving Body* has shrunk to a shallow pool of familiar bird-and-fish similes.

As this shrinkage of Lecoq's choral pedagogy indicates, the teaching of Greek choral dramaturgies in the UK overwhelmingly seeks to foreground concepts of unity and cohesion, even where such a focus might limit advanced/professional learners' opportunity for creative exploration and artistic self-determination. In recent years, concerns about the appearance of a limited 'canon' of accepted Lecoq pedagogy have been articulated, for example in Amy Russell's group interview 'Against the "Lecoq Canon"'. In the course of this discussion, Jonathan Young reflects: 'when the pedagogy is passed on to students and to the students of students, they can begin to mistake the curriculum for the pedagogy. They lose the spirit of inquiry and start to install a canon' (371). In many cases, the familiar drama studio exhortation to move like 'a flock of birds' or 'a shoal of fish' represents precisely this: the displacement of genuine pedagogic experiment with choral practices and presences in favour of a superficial appearance of harmonious co-creativity.

In the context of UK HE, such aspirations are frequently imbricated with a pervasive—if often inchoate—sense of tragedy as a rarefied, idealised, and spiritually elevating theatre-form. As Joshua Billings, Felix Budelmann, and Fiona Macintosh have written, modern receptions of ancient drama predominantly elect to position choral practices 'as harmoniously aligned with the cosmic, social, and political order' (4). However, in Chantal Mouffe's critical cultural analysis, the desire to conceptualise society as 'an harmonious and non-conflictual ensemble' (*On the Political* 10) characterises a 'post-political' (1–2) worldview 'unable to adequately grasp the pluralistic nature of the social world' and 'the conflicts that pluralism entails' (10). At the microcosmic level of drama studio choral pedagogy, a cognate situation may be observed. While UK HE's idealising conceptualisations of ancient theatre practice often enfold a valorisation of classical tragedy as somehow intertwined with the historical emergence of democratic politics,[5] they simultaneously serve to limit the scope of contemporary students to experience tragic dramaturgies as sites open to their own creative self-determination.

Actors-in-training learning to move in flock- and shoal-like ways are rarely required to respond with original critical intelligence to the subject-matter of the ancient plays they are working on. Instead, the mass reproduction of apparently spontaneous and frictionless choral choreographies denotes a training culture which wishes to absorb the cultural prestige of classical tragic plays as an apparently natural, apolitical inheritance, without engaging the qualities of embodied debate and contestation which regularly characterised the chorus-centred dramaturgies of fifth-century BCE Athens (Dunbar & Harrop 190–191). In their published form, Lecoq's tragic pedagogies hold space for multiple manifestations of choral agency, including those characteristic of a politically engaged, deliberative community. The chorus, he writes, 'may exhibit contradictions, its members may sometimes oppose one another in subgroups, or alternatively unite to address the public with one voice' (139). But students only presented with the miniaturised, 'flock-and-shoal' version of Lecoq's experimental pedagogy are denied such opportunities to conceptualise their choral selves as engaged and empowered creative and cultural agents.

However, as the remainder of this chapter will propose, this is not the only way in which Lecoq-inspired choral pedagogies can operate in relation to the drama studio teaching of Greek tragedy. The discussion which follows reflects the development of a personal teaching practice (my own),[6] rooted in the progressive emergence of new studio responses to principles and exercises laid out in *The Moving Body*. The resulting pedagogic practice responds strongly to Lecoq's foregrounding of spatial relationality between protagonist and chorus (137). It centres the creative interplay of 'balancing' and 'unbalancing' (141–142), taking these as catalysts for an emergent studio chorality characterised by playfulness, spontaneity, and spatial agency.[7] And it is alert to the potential of such practices for engaging and exploring agonistic energies within Greek tragic dramaturgy. Actively seeking alternatives to disempowering modern clichés of choral performance (erroneously understood by many actors-in-training, and sometimes their teachers, to represent historical truths), this approach aims to help students recognise themselves as culturally situated re-interpreters of classical drama, with both the capacity, and the creative authority, to re-imagine ancient theatre practices in a range of modes and moods, including those responsive to their own experiences of cultural or political dissensus.[8]

In tragic playwriting of the fifth-century BCE, the *agon* was a pair of speeches pitting diametrically opposed views against one another. The term was related to competitive sporting culture, where it could refer to the struggles and confrontations which took place in an athletic contest or wrestling match. Notions of agonism have been revived in contemporary political theory, primarily in Mouffe's formulations (*On the Political*; *The Democratic Paradox*; *Agonistics*)[9] where the term is used to describe a politics which challenges the pursuit of (neo)liberal consensus, insisting upon the necessity for ongoing processes of democratic debate and confrontation. Agonistic practice, Mouffe proposes, requires a pluralistic society to acknowledge, and openly choose between, the range of passionately held (and sometimes irreconcilable) positions occupied by its citizens. The aim is to 'mobilize those passions towards democratic designs' (*The Democratic Paradox* 103), rather than forcing dissenting voices beyond the margins of acceptable discourse. Mouffe's work identifies ongoing and impassioned 'agonistic struggle', rather than the pursuit of an illusory—and, in practice, often exclusionary—consensus, as 'the very condition of a vibrant democracy' (*Agonistics* 6–7). Drawing inspiration from these ideas, I have previously proposed the value of 're-conceptualizing Athenian tragedy as a form permeated by agonistic structures and practices', challenging 'prevalent notions of ancient tragedy as a catalyst for the creation of unified, consensual audience/communities', and instead 'asserting the critical importance of disunity, contention, and struggle' to the contemporary 'experience of tragedy' (Harrop 112–113).

In the context of the contemporary drama studio, such agonistic perspectives intersect provocatively with some of the essential principles of Lecoq-inspired pedagogy. Mouffe's political thinking envisages democratic practice as a rule-bound play of adversarial passions,[10] while Lecoq's famous emphasis on play (*le jeu*)[11] requires that performers cultivate a 'readiness to explore the circumstances of the moment', within 'a set of rules or expectations germane to the style or form of theatre under investigation' (Murray 50). Both formulations envisage essential (democratic or creative) freedoms as emerging in relation to an agreed set of rules, which confer structure and meaning upon passionate energies. And both position the practices they describe as open-ended, exploratory processes, rather than programmatic means towards pre-determined ends. In a late-life conversation with Dario Fo, Lecoq gave a sense of the intersection of political and artistic potential which facilitated his experiments in a newly liberated, postwar Europe: 'There were no more rules. We had to make up the game again' (Murray 14).[12] This discussion, Simon Murray suggests, 'reveals a strong feeling of optimism following the defeat of Fascism, and a sense that artists could—and should—empower themselves to invent afresh the rules of their particular creative work' (17). Although he never wished to frame his work as political,[13] Lecoq's pedagogies are infused with both a positive spirit of artistic agency and a pragmatic willingness to 'make up the game again' in response to changing circumstances and opportunities.

My own studio-based reimaginings of Lecoq-inspired pedagogies as prompts for agonistic choral experiment emerged over a decade, initially through successive misrememberings of, and classroom improvisations around, the exercise known as 'A Balanced Stage'.[14] In its classic (published) form, actors-in-training enter a stage, one by one, each choosing either to sustain or disrupt the spatial 'balance' already established by their peers. So, within the exercise, an actor might opt to take up a position which enhances an emerging sense of symmetry, or they might move in a way which deliberately 'unbalances' an existing pattern of bodies (Lecoq 141–143).[15] This first exercise then develops into a second, more complex, iteration, in which every new entrant temporarily assumes a 'weight' equal to that of all the other players combined, so that 'each new actor who comes on will cause those already on stage to regroup' (143–144). This version of the exercise also leads directly into the playful embodiment of tragic dynamics, as the final figure to enter the space 'will be the first hero, facing the first chorus' (144).[16]

My creative misremembering of these exercises was doubtless informed by my own encounters with the work of Complicité, especially their performances and workshops showcasing swift, playful choreographies created through dynamic flows of un-balancing and re-balancing space. Certainly, in my own studio pedagogy, a recurring game gradually crystallised in which a singular figure—metaphorically imbued with a 'weight' equal to that of the rest of the group combined—is given licence to disrupt the balancing-act being attempted by their peers. In the basic form of the game,[17] the singular figure is picked by the teacher/trainer. Sometimes, with more advanced groups, the protagonist has the option to pick their replacement via a game of 'tag' (the former protagonist immediately re-joining the co-operative collective). This accidental elaboration of the exercise adheres to tradition in building ensemble skills, encouraging heightened awareness, unspoken communication, and fluid collective motion. As with the classic version, it creates dynamic spatial configurations which can form the basis of scenic compositions. However, what is different in this version is that the rest of the group (the 'chorus') are expressly empowered to take collective action to mitigate the protagonist figure's wilful unbalancing of the space. They can resist. They can work proactively to defend their territory and values. And this slight shift brings into play an agonistic relationality between chorus and protagonist which diverges in some significant ways from Lecoq's conceptualisation of Greek tragedy.

In *The Moving Body*, Lecoq writes 'The shape of tragedy is marked by two main features: the chorus and the hero' (135). The former's role is to clear 'a space for tragedy' (139), into which a singular hero-figure will step. Morris explains the key relationships of Lecoq's tragic universe in this way: 'Fate is implacable. The laws of the Gods prevail. Heroes respect the laws, but passion, revenge or misadventure intervene, causing these laws to be broken. The Chorus keep to the laws of the Gods and accept Fate. These are the dynamics of Tragedy: Fate vs. Hero vs. Chorus' (151). In this account of classic Lecoq pedagogy, chorus and 'hero' engage in 'discourse', resulting in 'a constant shifting of balance to reflect their arguments' (151). However, there are also stated limits to this chorus' agency. Lecoq instructs that: 'the great rule governing the tragic chorus is never to be active, always reactive' (140).[18]

This is definitely not how it went with my own drama studio choruses who—given permission to playfully compete against the hero-protagonist—proved themselves capable of becoming skilled and spatially assertive theatrical players, collectively monitoring and managing the space of their interactions. They might even find moments to assert their collective agency, actively taking steps, within the playful parameters of the game, to defend their space against the risks posed by the disruptive presence of the singular hero-protagonist.[19] Once text is layered onto these spatial encounters, the outcome is a chorus with a strong sense of their collective presence and capacity, able to clear or cede space (as per Lecoq's formulations), but also to challenge or contest the destructively self-willed positions adopted by tragedy's singular hero-protagonists. Simon Goldhill has described 'the contrast between the collective chorus and the individual hero' as 'one of the structuring principles of tragedy' (47). In this view, 'the hero goes too far', making 'the boundaries of normal life problematic' (47):

> The hero is often destroyed—or destroys himself—in pursuit of his own goals, and this passionate self-belief and self-commitment is set in juxtaposition to the cooperative virtues of the community. (47)

Increasingly, our drama studio explorations of modified or Lecoq-inspired pedagogy began to probe what might happen if a chorus were to become conscious of their collective power to oppose (even occasionally to halt) such destructive displays of tragic individualism. Working in this way, student choruses can become active players in a game of embodied agonism, where a given drama's balance of personal and political loyalties is always in shifting, unpredictable spatial play.[20]

This sustained sense of play indicates another point of connection between agonistic experiment and Lecoq's legacies. As Mark Evans has outlined:

> Throughout his teaching, Lecoq exploits the overlap of meanings within the word 'play', allowing it to draw together associations with children's play, games and sports, as well as with acting and performance, all of which he allows to resonate within his pedagogy. (168)

Evans' work—together with that of Murray—has drawn attention to the importance of sport in the emergence of Lecoq's theatre pedagogies,[21] in ways which might offer valuable new provocations for studio explorations of tragic and choral acting. Turning the measured process of balancing the stage into a competitive game may run counter to some of Lecoq's premises concerning classical Greek aesthetics, but it also invites choral performers to invest their spatial play with 'the collective effort of the sports team', channelling their 'openness and intuitive responsiveness' towards shared goals (Evans 173). And although 'Lecoq never openly encouraged competition', Evans notes that he 'did not discourage the competitive atmosphere that would build up' in the course of his actor training. In Evans' judgment, Lecoq 'seemed to consider the tension, anticipation, energy and focus that it generated as beneficial for the quality of the students' work' (174). Perhaps tellingly, Lecoq's Paris school found its home in *Le Central* which had been 'a gymnasium devoted to boxing' (Murray 17), suggesting that a sense of embodied, agonistic struggle may not have been entirely alien to his conceptualisations of the actor's work.

In a similar way, infusing the teaching of Greek chorus with a spirit of competitive spatial play can lend a sense of immediacy, intention, and excitement. Creating a game which endows tragic choruses with active spatial agency raises the stakes of speeches and scene-studies, meaning that student actors in protagonist roles must work, moment-to-moment, to engage and maintain alliances with their physically engaged and assertive choral peers. In its foregrounding of spatial encounters and negotiations between the individual and the collective, or between different groups, this approach heightens the sense of tragedy as an agonistic theatre-form; its plots powered by irreconcilable differences of judgment and aspiration; and its embattled bodies permanently struggling to navigate contradictory currents of ethics, law, politics, inclusion, exclusion, alliance, vengeance, grief, and love.

Evans rightly cautions that: 'Sport, movement training and indeed even theatre itself are not, for Lecoq, essentially or primarily political' (168). Rather:

> [...] actions, gestures and movements left unfilled with intention (psychologically or politically) are then ready to participate in an exploration of theatrical and emotional dynamics in space in a manner that maximises the creative choices for the student and minimises the limitations on creative and imaginative play. (175)

However, Murray's evaluation of Lecoq's ongoing relevance is also apposite: 'his legacy will continue to be an open one, in which his ideas and practices are regularly given new life and different shape and are re-contextualised according to the circumstances of time and place' (159). Accordingly, this chapter has proposed that one important way in which the 'unfilled' form of Lecoq's balanced stage (and its variants) can generate meaningful imaginative play in relation to tragic drama is through the creation of space for embodying and exploring ancient plays' agonistic energies.

For emerging performers in present-day drama studios, pedagogic encounters with Greek tragedy are often understood as learning experiences in relation to which they have little or no intellectual and creative agency. Translated texts derived from ancient tragedy are frequently used to instil foundational principles of vocal and physical practice (Dunbar and Harrop 43–44), with the aim of producing disciplined, fluent, and ostensibly harmonious cohorts of learners. Across both drama school (conservatoire) and university programmes, practical experiences of classical drama are framed by de-contextualised and uncritical readings of Aristotle's *Poetics* (27), serving to reinforce many students' tacit learning that they lack the creative authority to interpret classical plays for themselves, and that 'a tragic play's meaning is singular, fixed, and non-negotiable' (45).[22] Almost universally, too, they are encouraged to emulate birds and fishes, creating an aesthetic display of de-politicised, apparently spontaneous consensus which is vaguely supposed to correspond to tragedy's status as a serene, unchanging, and idealised cultural form, but which might more accurately be read as corresponding to deep-seated (neo)liberal anxieties about the potential consequences of allowing students' diverse experiences and aspirations to inform their explorations of high-status ancient plays. However, this chapter has contended that it is worth attending to Lecoq's description of tragedy as 'the greatest form of theatre that is still open to renewal' (135), and his insistence that: 'Far from taking an historical view of ancient tragedy and its imagined codes of communication, we seek to reinvent the tragic form for today' (135).

In this spirit, the pedagogic experiments described in this chapter set out to endow learners with the 'confidence to play imaginatively and creatively' (Murray 103), preparing them to engage as active, embodied agents in relation to a theatre-form which recurrently stages unresolved disputes and confrontations emerging from the most challenging cultural, ethical, and political territories. Beginning from processes of collective spatial play and proceeding to embed playful forms of physical contest and confrontation as foundations of a tragic dramaturgy, this work seeks to re-position the acting of tragedy as an explicitly agonistic process of co-creative, ethically engaged, and imaginative citizenship. As Billings, Budelmann, and Macintosh observe, the Greek chorus is a phenomenon perennially open to imaginative transformation, 'appealed to, longed for, or imagined' (5) in a variety of forms. This chapter offers a reimagining of choral practice in the drama studio as an experience which invites learners to bring their whole (embodied and intellectual) selves to the process of reinventing ancient drama's confrontations and struggles, fusing Lecoq-inspired choral pedagogy with an agonistic conception of tragedy to bring classical dramaturgies into new creative conjunction with students' contemporary experiences, commitments, struggles, and aspirations.

Notes

1 'I was to play a role so important it was the name of the play—Lysistrata in *Lysistrata*, and my year were really happy for me. We only later found out this performance wouldn't be on Silk Street, it would be in South London; a 35-minute drive across the river. My mates were sad. They hugged me. "No agent is going to come to this, Michaela. Not the hot ones. They simply won't cross the river".' (47–48). Coel does not discuss the fact that, in UK theatre culture, ancient comedy is often understood to be less prestigious than tragedy. But in such a context, this casting also raises important questions concerning the kinds of classical texts and roles that global majority of actors-in-training are able to lay claim to.
2 The drama school in question has since issued a public apology for some of the incidents Coel and her peers have drawn attention to (Coel 42–43; Harrison).

3 Prior to this publication, a range of concepts and practices had been disseminated via theatre artists who had studied with Lecoq. See Eastman 363–364.
4 A companion resource on '7 Levels of Tension' does acknowledge Lecoq as a source of inspiration. Both may be found at: www.actorsofdionysus.com/education/free-resources. Accessed 22 June 2022.
5 The arguments are considered more fully in Harrop (100).
6 This work took place at a number of institutions, especially Rose Bruford College of Theatre and Performance and The Royal Central School of Speech and Drama. I am deeply grateful to all the students I worked with during those years for their creative courage, and spirit of critical contestation.
7 This sits within a wider conceptualisation of tragedy as: 'a serious play on a mythic or heroic theme (incorporating a sizeable dose of suffering, grief, or anguish), containing music and dance, its dramaturgy rooted in interactions between individual actors and a collective chorus' (Dunbar and Harrop 11). This final part of this formulation is in turn indebted to Goldhill (46–53).
8 Thanks are due to TaPRA's Performer Training Working Group for their feedback on an earlier version of this discussion. Also to Marcus Louch, who supported preliminary research for that paper while undertaking a Summer Research Scholarship at Liverpool Hope University.
9 See also Fisher and Katsouraki.
10 See, for instance, Mouffe, *On the Political* 20–21; 32–33; 52.
11 On 'play' in Lecoq's pedagogy, and its legacies, see Coletto and Buckley 112–118.
12 The conversation quoted by Murray originally appears in Jean-Gabriel Roy and Jean-Noël Carasso's film *Le deux voyages a Jacques Lecoq* (1999). See also Murray 39–40.
13 On his role in 'the "denazification" of Germany' see Lecoq 5.
14 On the genealogy of this exercise see Morris 153–154.
15 See also Morris 151.
16 Lecoq uses the term 'hero' for this figure. In my own practice, I prefer the term 'protagonist', which in addition to being more inclusive, contains the stem *agon*, recalling the argumentative and competitive function of the ancient tragic actor. In this discussion, the composite 'hero-protagonist' is sometimes deployed to indicate thinking drawing on both traditions.
17 This appears in *Greek Tragedy and the Contemporary Actor* under the title 'Protagonist v. Chorus' (Dunbar and Harrop 175–176).
18 In *The Moving Body*, Lecoq presupposes a sustained physical distance between the chorus and a tragedy's protagonists, taking as a given the (possibly Hellenistic) principle that 'the Greek chorus was not on the same level of the actors' (140).
19 There are resonances here with Murray's Exercise 4.7 (part of 'Towards the Dynamics of Tragedy', 141), although Murray's discussion is strongly informed by the idea of tragedy's actors as driven by external forces: successive exercises embed the sense that 'forces stronger than yourself are provoking you' (145).
20 Compare Morris 151.
21 On receptions of 'Ancient Greek physical culture' in Lecoq training see Evans 148.
22 For a fuller account of this critique, see Dunbar and Harrop 27–49.

Works Cited

Billings, Joshua, Felix Budelmann, and Fiona Macintosh, editors. *Choruses, Ancient and Modern*. Oxford University Press, 2013.

Callery, Dymphna. *Through the Body: A Practical Guide to Physical Theatre*. Nick Hern, 2001.

Cavendish, Dominic. 'Sixties Permissiveness Created a Culture Open to Abuse at Drama Schools.' *The Telegraph*, 31 May 2021, www.telegraph.co.uk/theatre/what-to-see/sixties-permissiveness-created-culture-open-abuse-drama-schools. Accessed 20 June 2022.

Cavendish, Dominic, and Susannah Goldsbrough. 'Exclusive: Drama Schools that Launched some of Britain's National Treasures Accused of Sexual Harassment.' *The Telegraph*, 31 May 2021, https://www.telegraph.co.uk/news/2021/05/31/exclusive-drama-schools-launched-britains-national-treasures . Accessed 20 June 2022.

Coel, Michaela. *Misfits: A Personal Manifesto*. Ebury, 2021.

Coletto, Paola, and Jennifer Buckley. 'What Works and What Doesn't Work: On Play.' *The Routledge Companion to Jacques Lecoq*, edited by Mark Evans and Rick Kemp, Routledge, 2016, 112–118.

Cornford, Tom. *Theatre Studios: A Political History of Ensemble Theatre-Making*. Routledge, 2020.

Dryburgh, Jamieson. 'Approaching Pedagogical Arts Research from within the Studio.' *Theatre, Dance and Performance Training* 13.4 (2022): 536–553.

Dunbar, Zachary, and Stephe Harrop. *Greek Tragedy and the Contemporary Actor*. Palgrave, 2018.

Eastman, Helen. 'Chorus in Contemporary British Theatre.' *Choruses, Ancient and Modern*, edited by Joshua Billings, Felix Budelmann and Fiona Macintosh, Oxford University Press, 2013, 363–336.

Evans, Mark. 'The Influence of Sports on Jacques Lecoq's Actor Training.' *Theatre, Dance and Performance Training* 3.2 (2012): 163–177.

Evans, Mark. 'Playing with History: Personal Accounts of the Political and Cultural Self in Actor Training Through Movement.' *Theatre, Dance and Performance Training* 5.2 (2014): 144–156.

Fisher, Tony, and Eve Katsouraki, editors. *Performing Antagonism: Theatre, Performance & Radical Democracy*. Palgrave, 2017.

Goldhill, Simon. *How to Stage Greek Tragedy Today*. University of Chicago Press, 2007.

Harrison, Ellie. 'Drama School Guildhall Apologises to Paapa Essiedu and Michaela Coel for "Appalling" Racism.' *The Independent*, 10 June 2022, www.independent.co.uk/arts-entertainment/tv/news/paapa-essiedu-guildhall-racism-b2098444.html. Accessed 18 July 2022.

Harrop, Stephe. 'Greek Tragedy, Agonistic Space, and Contemporary Performance.' *New Theatre Quarterly* 34.2 (2018): 99–114.

Heddon, Dee, and Jane Milling. *Devising Performance: A Critical History*. Palgrave, 2006.

Hodge, Ali, editor. *Actor Training*. 2nd ed. Routledge, 2010.

Lecoq, Jacques. *The Moving Body: Teaching Creative Theatre*. Translated by David Bradby. Methuen, 2002.

Giannachi, Gabriella, and Mary Luckhurst. *On Directing: Interviews with Directors*. Faber, 1999.

Morris, Shona. 'The Chorus.' *The Routledge Companion to Jacques Lecoq*, edited by Mark Evans and Rick Kemp, Routledge, 2016, 150–156.

Mouffe, Chantal. *On the Political*. Routledge, 2005.

———. *The Democratic Paradox*. Verso, 2005.

———. *Agonistics: Thinking the World Politically*. Verso, 2013.

Murray, Simon. *Jacques Lecoq*. Routledge, 2003.
Rogers, Jami. 'Diversity School Redacted Report', 2021, www.issuu.com/dsicompany/docs/diversity_school_redacted_report. Accessed 20 June 2022.
Russell, Amy. 'Against the "Lecoq Canon".' *Theatre, Dance and Performance Training* 11.3 (2020): 370–377.
Yossman, K.J. 'Leading British Drama Schools Facing Allegations of Sexual Harassment, Abuse' *Variety*, 1 June 2021, www.variety.com/2021/film/global/british-drama-school-sexual-harassment-1234985365. Accessed 13 Mar. 2022.

6 The Pedagogic Value of Participating in a Chorus

Helen Eastman and Alex Silverman

What can performers gain from participation in a dramatic chorus? For a group of individuals to speak, sing, and move together, training is inevitably required. In 5th-century BCE Athens, where theatre emerged from the tradition of choral singing and dancing, this experience of training with one's fellow citizens (and in some cases with those of different social status or from further afield) was thought to contribute not just to the creation of works of art, but to the development and expression of both the individual and the wider community.[1] This is arguably an idealised view of a practice which was not homogenous, but as complex and diverse as the dramatic repertoire of ancient Greece, and the many people who performed and watched it. Nonetheless, its essential precept—that training for the chorus equips participants for other areas of their lives—may well apply to modern performers as well as their ancient forebears. In this chapter, we test this idea with reference to three long-term projects and their learning outcomes; we ask whether our practical experience of making choruses for the modern stage can help us to reflect in a more nuanced way on theatrical practice in antiquity; and we contextualise our findings in current discussions of participation in theatre studies.

We approach this from the perspective of theatre makers who are also classicists. In our long collaboration as director and composer, chorus-centred productions have accounted for more than half of our output. Moreover, as scholars who are actively engaged in the teaching and performance of ancient drama, we welcome this opportunity to challenge idealised and outdated notions of the chorus as intrinsically democratic or, like the tradition which promotes such an idea, essentially exclusive. While much of our work has concerned the performance of ancient drama in the original language, in this instance, we are not limiting ourselves to either choruses or pedagogical outcomes that pertain specifically to classical Greek drama.[2] As in the ancient world, our choruses have found audiences beyond the theatre: our examples include performances on film, online, at community meetings, and at international business conferences; we also make reference to works in English, and choruses that incorporate texts in French, Louisiana Creole, and Haida. As such our definition of chorus is broad and encompasses many different

DOI: 10.4324/b22844-8

performance events where individuals perform as a choral unit. Accordingly, we hope to reflect critically upon the chorus as we have encountered it: a theatrical technique which has consensual participation at its core.

Chorus is not frequently mentioned in the interrogation of participation by theatre scholars, who have documented the blurring of boundaries between audience and performer in modern theatrical practice, and considered its political implications.[3] They tell us that: in the modern theatre ecology performers and audiences alike seek agency through participation in drama and have high expectations of shaping their own experiences of theatre and the stories told there;[4] that participating in performance remains an effective means to engage in public discourse, although increased access to participation does not necessarily correlate to a greater chance of building consensus (Harrop, 112–113); and that while participatory performance can certainly empower individuals to find their voice, it may also be used to reinforce existing power structures (Jeffers, 218). From this brief overview, we may infer that the modern stage remains a place where performers can learn to express themselves, to debate with one another, and to define their relationships to institutions. Before we assess the extent to which these outcomes might be observed in our own work, it is worth considering the range of other benefits which are thought to have derived from choral participation in its original form.

The social function of the ancient theatrical chorus has been widely discussed.[5] To consider the chorus explicitly as a locus for pedagogy, we could do worse than to revisit the 'Old Oligarch', for whom choral performance stands alongside three other foundational Athenian activities: participation in games, manning of triremes, and service in the jury ([Xen.] *Ath. Pol.* 1.13). The chorus would have been an apt training ground for each of these tasks. It gave participants the experience of performing before a large crowd, and a taste of friendly competition; learning to dance with a chorus requires fitness, physical aptitude, and the ability to follow and retain instruction; participation in the city's festivals gave choreuts—those recruited to perform in the chorus—an ownership of their shared culture and values, and a forum in which to discuss them; choral practice required engagement in moral debate and the appreciation of oratory. That these skills were viewed as more than incidental benefits is borne out in the way chorus training was funded. Choruses were provided for by the system of liturgy, a tax levied from the wealthiest citizens to fund public services such as the upkeep of gymnasia or triremes, and festivals. In this respect, Barbara Kowalzig tells us, 'dancing in the khoros was perceived as contributing as much to the running of the polis as any of the other jobs that made up the much-invoked democratic way of life' (39).

The chorus was, then, seen as an ideal way to mould Athenian citizens, equipping them with skills which could be applied not just in the theatre, but in the community. In the following brief case studies, we explore how this may also be true for modern performers, and the pedagogical outcomes that have arisen in our joint interaction with dramatic choruses.

Learning to Learn Together: Choruses in the Cambridge Greek Plays 2010–2016

The skills needed by choreuts on the ancient stage were not dissimilar to those needed by 'triple-threat' performers in modern musical theatre: singing, dancing, and acting. Despite the fact that the chorus often has more material and stage time than the protagonists, they are often less experienced performers: they are still learning their craft and the choral rehearsal room can be an effective place for choral participants to learn *how* to work, and to work at the art of learning. While the ancient rehearsal room is a sadly underexplored topic, this assertion was certainly borne out in our experience of training student choruses for the Cambridge Greek Plays from 2010 to 2016.[6]

We worked with 46 students over three intensive phases of workshop, rehearsal, and production[7] on five plays—*Agamemnon* (2010) and *Prometheus Bound* (2013) by Aeschylus, *Frogs* (2013) and *Lysistrata* (2016) by Aristophanes, and *Antigone* (2013) by Sophocles—featuring choruses of Argive, Theban and Athenian elders, angry landladies, poetry fanatics, Nereids, protesting wives, sex-starved Spartans, and dancing frogs. As well as singing, dancing and acting, and delivering text in ancient Greek, our choruses were coached in Greek meter, clowning, improvisation, choral movement, circus skills, clog-dancing, and the ukulele.

Of course, it would have proved impossible to cast a ready-made troupe proficient in all those skills.[8] The length and breadth of the list given above confirms two things: participation in the chorus presupposes a process of training and learning new skills; and no two participants' learning journeys will be the same, as the effective casting of a chorus comprises recruiting candidates who have some of the necessary skills, and the aptitude to learn others. To this end, the recruitment process must also take account of how individual performers will impact the training of the whole group and have among its priorities the selection of chorus members who are well-placed to learn with and from each other.

In the case of the Cambridge Greek Plays, all participants—even the Classics students, who typically make up less than half the chorus—are required to improve their language skills. With Greek drama in the original language come the additional challenges of lyric meter. Many students came in with not just a limited understanding of the workings of Greek lyric meter, but a genuine wariness of it; being made to chant and sing the rhythms of the choral odes repeatedly became an opportunity to reassess an element of the Greek language which they had previously found difficult. In the classroom, meter can be presented as a puzzle to be solved, and so become a barrier to the understanding of the choral passages. In the rehearsal room, meter is a tool for achieving one of the most daunting tasks that faces any group of choral performers—the memorisation of hundreds of lines. By imposing apparent order on an otherwise daunting string of alien sounds, it can act as a bridge to mastery of performance in a foreign language. Meter also becomes a point of connection for all members of that group as the rhythm of the verse necessitates the synchronisation of breath, and so invites coordinated physical response to a text. This experience can be unifying, breed confidence and offer invaluable help to an amateur chorus training to perform before their peers. This process, then sheds light on the composition of plays in antiquity, the relationship between their form and rehearsal process, the centrality of meter in that process and the other transferable skills which might emerge from engagement with lyric meter.

The example of choral response to meter is an apt demonstration of the negotiation that occurs in every aspect of choral performance, in which the skills of the individual are secondary to the accomplishment of the whole group. It reminds us that a chorus is best considered not only in terms of its end product—the performance—but as an inherently pedagogic process. The skills required to empower a group of individuals to perform as one coherent whole are built in a rehearsal room: for singing and dancing (or juggling or unicycling or even speaking for that matter) to occur, choral participants are required to practice leadership and ductility, trust and interdependence.

Spaces and Places: Choruses in Barefaced Greek Films, 2019–2022

While our Cambridge choruses trained and performed in the town where they were living, before an audience of their peers, in the context of a performance tradition continuously associated with that place for over a century, our recent projects for Barefaced Greek ventured further afield, telling old stories in a new medium and taking choral performers far beyond their familiar environment. Two choral films, of the first stasimon in *Antigone* and the dawn chorus from Euripides' fragmentary tragedy *Phaethon*, were both shot on location in Greece using participants from the University of British Columbia's *Go Global* programme.[9] Of these, only two had studied Classics, and few had encountered their fellow participants or left Canada before; both cohorts contained students who had not previously left their home province.

The films were shot over a few days in 2018 and 2022, in the middle of longer tours of cultural and archaeological sites. This unconventional process precipitated unforeseen outcomes, as elements of the films we were making and the physical journey the students had embarked upon mirrored each other; we had to build a chorus who would not only perform together but also travel together to a new and different place. On their trip they were responding to Greece not as individual travellers but as a collective. The skills learned in rehearsal prompted them not just to stand and observe ancient artefacts, but to engage physically and collectively with them. Specifically, we worked on a 'flocking' technique, a form of choral movement which imitates the flow and formation of birds or fish.[10] The results of this work feature for a few fleeting seconds in the finished films (see Figure 6.1); but our UBC colleagues, who

74 *Helen Eastman and Alex Silverman*

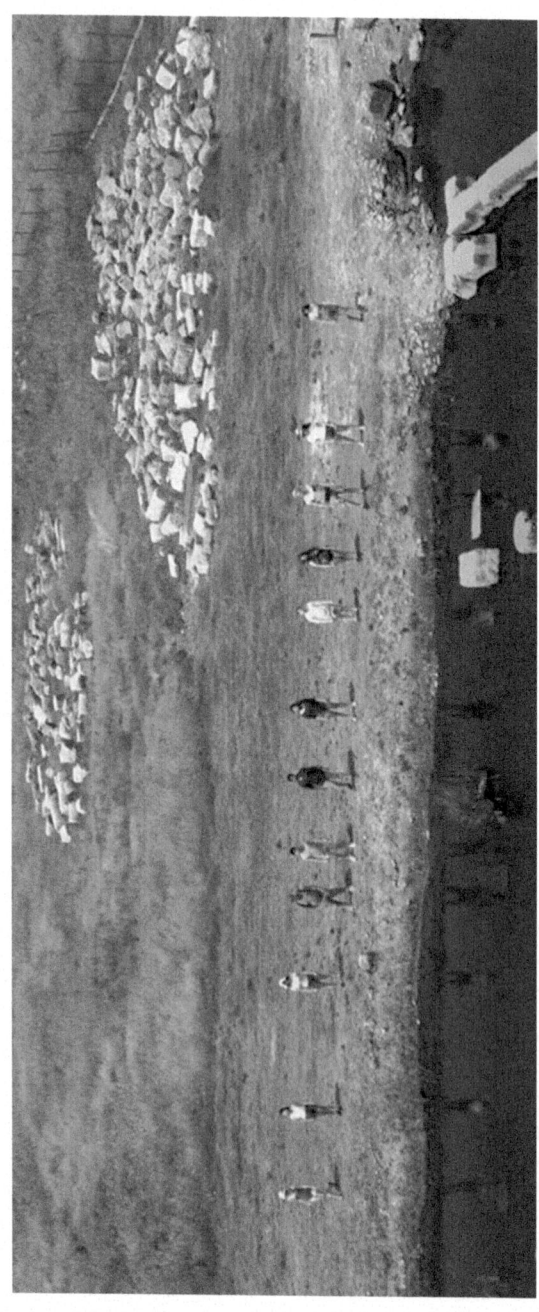

Figure 6.1 The chorus of *Antigone* find themselves in formation at the archaeological site of Oiniades. Photograph: Michael Garrett.

chaperoned the students on the remainder of the trip, reported that the group found an opportunity to practice this technique at every ancient site visited, and on every day before and after the filming. Working chorally around ancient ruins changed not only the way the chorus moved, but what they noticed in the landscape: in discussion between takes the participants pointed out the arrangement of houses in a village, the movement of birds and goats, the way wind turbines line up on the hill—groupings which, in turn, they would later attempt to imitate and integrate into their own choral movement. These patterns, tracing associations between landscape and performers, are fundamental to both films.

The effect of the practice of choral movement could also be observed in more mundane moments: a chorus who learn to move together develops the skills to collaborate without a leader, and to navigate spaces, such as an airport or beach, as a group. The work enhanced participants' ability to work together, allowing them to move film kit and suitcases with surprisingly little discussion, argument, or injury. For us, this is a salient reminder that skills learned in the rehearsal room are applicable far beyond the formal space of a theatre, or a film location: they resonate as performers go out, together and separately into the wider world. With this in mind, we may reconsider the applications of the physical aspects of choral training in ancient society. There is no suggestion that an Athenian choreut would practice combat in preparation for a dramatic performance; however, it stands to reason that they may have emerged from their time in the chorus better prepared to learn and execute the skills required of a soldier.

A third film made for Barefaced Greek during the Covid pandemic placed choral participants in almost the opposite situation.[11] In our *Oedipus* chorus, the challenge was to construct a sense of chorality from participants who were recording separately in their homes. Instead of responding chorally to a new environment, our lockdown chorus was invited to reengage with the homes they had been stuck in for long periods of time. The film explores how our relationships with our domestic environments can be transformed when seen in the context of people in other spaces. One moment of choreography in this piece (led by Abi Rosser) asked the chorus to engage—together, but apart—with a chair in their own home, challenging them to find beauty and purpose in something often overlooked and to forge a choral identity while never meeting, using their diverse bodies, personal effects, and private space (see Figure 6.2). This chorus, who worked to achieve uniformity from their own homes, are an intriguing counterexample to the much-discussed concept of a chorus as a vehicle for playing out arguments in a public space.[12] Mastery of this moment required participants to exercise generosity and self-awareness, arguably in a different way and to a greater degree than in an orthodox rehearsal environment. This example demonstrates clearly how pedagogical outcomes of such work are mitigated by performance context. Their success is in large part dependent on the participants themselves: the most interesting

76 *Helen Eastman and Alex Silverman*

Figure 6.2 The masked *Oedipus* chorus dances on their chairs. Images captured by performers from the Live Canon ensemble.

work happens when members of a chorus encounter each other, and see their own experience reflected and shaped by their peers.

Discourse, Dissemination, and Dissent: Choruses in *Foreclosure Follies* and *Risk!*, 2016–2023

The examples given above, of work in Cambridge and for Barefaced Greek, have two essential elements in common: ancient dramatic source texts delivered in the original language, and groups of participants who have some shared identity outside of their work together in the chorus—as students in the same institution, residents of the same town, or citizens living under similar restrictions at a time of global pandemic. Our final set of case studies feature choruses drawn deliberately from further afield—from different countries and cultures, from different social backgrounds and with vastly different life experiences.

Foreclosure Follies and *Risk!* resulted from a long collaboration between the authors and Janis Sarra, a distinguished Canadian professor of law and campaigner, exploring institutional accountability in the aftermath of the global financial crash, and financial risk in the face of the climate crisis. Sarra was interested not only in the way that choral techniques could bring her work to a wider audience but also more vividly into focus for corporate stakeholders and others already engaged with these issues. Sarra's academic papers were the starting point, although not the entire text, for both productions.[13] We worked with a chorus, including professional performers, but also lawyers, economists, financiers, insurance brokers, judges, and academics to make cabaret shows which explored the issues in approachable ways—through song, sketches, poetry, and choral performance.[14]

Each scene was generated through a process of open discussion, prompted by Sarra's research. Performers asked questions, and experts shared their perspectives. We synthesised these conversations to create a choral text which reflected everyone in the room and would be accessible to a non-expert audience while remaining impactful for experts in the field. An early chorus, entitled *Who's at the table?*, which in the final script amounts to some 20 lines, was the result of a 3-hour discussion on the need for clarity in financial regulation, a matter on which some chorus members had differing expert opinions, and others were ignorant. The complexities around enfranchisement—being 'at the table' or being 'other'—were highlighted by the fact that our performers included people, in terms of financial decision-making, sat at vastly different positions at, and distances from the metaphorical table. This piece required each participant to hear and understand each other's points of view, and then to stand together and express them in public. Achieving consent around a mutually agreeable performance text took empathy and open-mindedness on all sides; the process of sharing in a creative decision-making process, and performing its results alongside participants with a different, even opposing world-view was arguably of greater value than the piece of art that resulted. The creation of choral work, especially where there is not a pre-existing or fixed text, is an excellent arena for learning to compromise. To this extent, the devising process which generated *Foreclosure Follies* relied upon the agonistic potential of the chorus and the space in which it operates.[15]

This highlights a foundational question with resonance for all contemporary and ancient choral performance: whom do the chorus represent? When performers join together to work as one body, they necessarily subjugate aspects of their own identity to that of the chorus. Our lockdown chorus showed how this is possible even when performers are physically far apart. In the case of the *Foreclosure Follies*, the distance between performers was ideological. Choral performance forces participants to address questions about who they are in relation to each other, and to an audience.

This example speaks to the relationships of individuals within a choral group, but this work also showed that chorus can also be a tool for defining relationships of an individual *to* a group. Our starting point had been text written for an academic readership, not for performance. Performing that text with a chorus required adaptations not just of medium but of voice. For Sarra, as an author, that meant handing over the text to a group, and accepting that the group would take ownership of it and deliver it in a completely different way (perhaps even singing it). This process is complex and requires trust. It is predicated on the hope that others may find a more effective means of communicating your own message.

We reflected that process structurally by beginning both pieces with the individual academic voice, in the style of a lecture. In *Foreclosure Follies*, we disrupted that voice, allowing the lone lecturer to be drowned out by a dissenting chorus (see Figure 6.3); in *Risk!*, we amplified that single voice, drawing the chorus into the lecture as backing singers. In both cases, the moment of transition, the point at which a single voice gives way to a choral performance, is the point at which the content becomes demonstrably more accessible. While the underlying message remains the same, the chorus has greater power to attract an audience. In an age when individualism in public discourse is viewed with scepticism, much as it was in classical Athens, dislike or mistrust of a speaker can undermine the content of a speech. Text delivered by a chorus is often far harder to dismiss: a group of performers, although by no means impossible to dislike, is at once more relatable and less knowable than many of the individuals with whom they interact on stage. From this we draw some lessons: that effective communication is often predicated upon a decision about voice; that one person's message may be conveyed more powerfully in another's voice; that this effect can be compounded when those voices speak together; and that putting words in the mouths of a chorus requires trust and negotiation.

Of course, we should not pretend that such negotiations are always smooth or successful. Preparing a chorus can be difficult, and consensus on that

Pedagogic Value of Participating in Chorus 79

Figure 6.3 Janis Sarra's lecture on corporate financial responsibility is drowned out by a dissenting chorus. Photograph: Michael Garrett.

journey is not a given. When risks are taken, and human participants involved, there will inevitably be failures of communication too. We have learned that in choral work there must always be space for dissent—from consensus, and from chorality itself. Without this possibility, little of value can be created or negotiated. For us, this was borne out in a performance of *Risk!* in 2022. The centrepiece of the show is a song called *Time for hope*:[16] the entire audience are invited to join in with singing its simple refrain, and if they feel bold enough to do so, to step forward and read out a personal pledge to take environmental action. A group of high-profile lawyers and finance professionals had agreed to participate in the show before an audience of their peers in Toronto—this is an obvious strategy for forging a connection between chorus and audience and had worked effectively for us in previous performances in corporate environments. Each of our guests learned their part diligently and contributed gamely to our rehearsals. So when some of them approached us, minutes before going on stage, and announced that they felt uncomfortable giving public voice to their personal pledges, requesting that actors from our company should read them out instead, thus avoiding the risk of being witnessed in the act of participation, we were faced with a decision. In that (alarming) moment, we felt strongly that delegating the act of reading a personal statement to another performer was a dereliction of the commitment to their otherwise admirable pledges and represented an unacceptable level of disengagement from a performance that depended on communal, choral activity. The show went ahead, and we performed the song, but omitted our guests' contributions. Other participants within the group who had made their own pledges in the song felt intensely let down by this refusal to commit, and with some justification. Nevertheless, this moment is instructive. It reminds us that the chorus must be considered not only in terms of its product, the moment of performance: there is more to be learned by observing chorus as a process, and one which may as likely be characterised by dissent among its participants—from each other, even from chorality itself—as by the consent required to act together.

Conclusions

These three case studies give a sense of the vast potential of choral participation as a pedagogical tool. In broad terms, we may assert that, much as it was reported to have been in antiquity, training to perform with a dramatic chorus today remains an effective way to engage with wider society, physically and politically, and morally; and that, in common with other forms of participatory theatre, choral performance is an apt medium in which to develop and investigate questions of authorship, agonism, and the assertion of corporate identity. It is also much more: the chorus offers participants opportunities to improve the way they learn and to apply their learning in new ways. As the chorus is increasingly expected to do more than just act, sing, and move, it is often the locus and catalyst for the acquisition and sharing of other skills. Choral participants learn new ways of looking at their environment, and of conducting themselves within it; they often find an avenue not just to attain authorship, but to share it; and in the act of training and performing as one body with their peers, they are likely to encounter and learn new, productive ways to express diversity of opinion and disagreement.

None of the above outcomes is guaranteed or universal—they are dependent on context. A chorus' experience is shaped by the other creative practitioners with whom they interact. To this extent, while choruses are often empowered to make decisions as a group, they frequently remain subject to the vision of a director or writer—as artists we are especially mindful of this responsibility. It seems absurd to describe any dramatic chorus as 'democratic'. Nonetheless, we have found dramatic choral performance to be a form of expression and a learning opportunity that is readily accessible and adaptable to participants of any background or skill set. The wider circumstances of a production will always impact on the time and training available, and so on the pedagogical potential of any chorus: we should acknowledge that all but one of the cases we have discussed in this chapter had some degree of funding or support from academic institutions, which both enabled effective training opportunities for choral participants and to some extent raised the expectation of positive learning outcomes. Even so, we assert that these opportunities and outcomes are transferrable to productions in other contexts, both in professional theatre and in community projects, precisely because of the persistent and unique feature of a chorus—its participant members, and the set of relationships that they form with each other when rehearsing and performing.

Notes

1 Plato's assertion (*Leg.* 654a–b) that the person who has no experience of the chorus (*achoreutos*) is uneducated is the most frequently cited evidence for the chorus as a locus of instruction. Vernant's description of the chorus as a 'college of citizens' is telling and typical of 20th-century understanding of the ancient chorus (33–34). See Peponi for an overview of some of the perceived benefits of Athenian choral training (21–22). In respect of non-citizen participation, Jackson argues persuasively that 'for drama and its choruses the requirement for citizenship could well have been less intrinsic for the selection process' (31).
2 On stage: *Agamemnon* (2010), *Prometheus Bound* (2013), *Frogs* (2013), *Antigone* (2016), and *Lysistrata* (2016), all for the Cambridge Greek Play at Cambridge Arts Theatre; the original iteration of *Foreclosure Follies* (2016) included a single chorus in ancient Greek. On film: *Ode to Man* (2019), *Oedipus Chorus* (2021), and *Phaethon Dawn Chorus* (2023), all for Barefaced Greek. For further insight into the pedagogical Greek Play tradition, see Peter Swallow's chapter in this volume.
3 See especially Harpin and Nicholson. Matarasso offers a practitioner's viewpoint.
4 For an examination of the extent to which modern theatre relies on 'productive participation' by audience members, see Alston.
5 In antiquity this discussion plays out in Plato's *Laws* and Aristotle's *Poetics*. Weiner addresses this subject directly and concisely; Havelock insists that the chorus is

where language is taught and developed. Among recent perspectives, see Jackson on synergies with military training (205–207); contrastingly, Scullion is sceptical that the chorus could be useful in preparing citizens for actual combat (134). Goldhill makes the case for chorus as a tool for creating social cohesion (252–253).

6 On ancient rehearsals, see Marshall. The discussion of the Cambridge Greek Play here provides an instructive parallel to Peter Swallow's discussion in this volume of the annual King's College London project.

7 In terms of basic measurable outcomes, it seems worth noting that alumni of the Greek Plays in these years, some of whom had never previously been on stage, went on to train at LAMDA, East 15, Mountview, ALRA, Juilliard, The Actors' Studio NY, Central School of Speech and Drama, and Drama Studio London, and are still working in the industry.

8 Furthermore, it bears pointing out that while Cambridge has a thriving drama scene, and a tradition of performance of ancient plays dating back to 1882 (on which see Easterling), it has no theatre department or actual drama students. This fact has never diminished the ambition of the show's producers or directors; it does underscore the importance of a more general skills-training as part of choral rehearsal.

9 Both films can be viewed on YouTube. *Ode to man* is a complete performance of ll.332–375 of *Antigone* (https://www.youtube.com/watch?v=f5PNz-aPKoE). Only some 400 lines of *Phaethon* remain: the *Dawn Chorus*, ll.63–101 is the play's only complete extant choral ode (https://www.youtube.com/watch?v=ZJRTJ7zFsv8). UBC's *Go Global* programme is funded by the Canadian Arts Research Award, and offers opportunities for undergraduates to travel and study abroad. The focus of this particular course was to 'explore ancient Greek drama beyond the confines of the traditional classroom by associating texts with particular sites in Greece and ancient performance traditions and conventions' ('GO GLOBAL 2019').

10 This technique, among others, is discussed in more detail in Helen Eastman's earlier reflections on the application of Lecoq's choral techniques in drama schools (364–365). See also Stephe Harrop's discussion of this exercise in this volume.

11 Online at https://www.youtube.com/watch?v=x709ixKqpoE

12 See Harrop, and our discussion of the dissenting chorus below. On public space in ancient theatre see Wiles, *Tragedy in Athens* and *A Short History*.

13 Among others: Sarra, 'An opportune moment', 'The anthropocene', *From Ideas to Action*, and Sarra and Wade.

14 *Foreclosure Follies* and *Risk!* were made with support from the Peter Wall institute of UBC and the Canada Climate Law Initiative. They have been performed on 9 separate occasions in Canada, the United States, the United Kingdom, and in Greece since 2016, and precipitated two further choral performance projects. The original production is documented at https://www.livecanon.co.uk/special-projects/foreclosurefollies

15 For a deeper exploration of this idea, see Harrop.

16 A version of this song, recorded by participants on several continents during the COVID pandemic is available to view on YouTube at https://www.youtube.com/watch?v=uvaz7C3MTtw

Works Cited

Alston, Adam. *Beyond Immersive Theatre: Aesthetics, Politics, and Productive Participation*. Palgrave Macmillan, 2016.

Easterling, Pat. 'The Early Years of the Cambridge Greek Play: 1883–1912.' *Classics in 19th and 20th Century Cambridge: Curriculum, Culture and Community*, edited by Christopher Stray, Cambridge Philological Society, 1998, 27–47.

Eastman, Helen. 'Chorus in Contemporary British Theatre.' *Choruses, Ancient and Modern*, edited by Joshua Billings, et al., Oxford University Press, 2013, 363–376.

'GO GLOBAL 2019 led by Professor Hallie Marshall: Go to Greece to Study Ancient Greek Drama!' *University of British Columbia*, 2019, https://theatrefilm.ubc.ca/news/go-global-2019-led-by-professor-hallie-marshall-go-to-greece-to-study-ancient-greek-drama. Accessed 25 Aug. 2023.

Goldhill, Simon. 'Collectivity and Otherness—The Authority of the Tragic Chorus: Response to Gould.' *Tragedy and the Tragic: Greek Theatre and Beyond*, edited by Michael Silk, Clarendon Press, 1996, 244–256.

Havelock, Eric A. 'The oral Composition of Greek Drama.' *Quaderni Urbinati Di Cultura Classica* 6 (1980): 61–113.

Harpin, Anna, and Helen Nicholson, editors. *Performance and Participation: Practices, Audiences, Politics*. Palgrave Macmillan, 2016.

Harrop, Stephe. 'Greek Tragedy, Agonistic Space, and Contemporary Performance.' *New Theatre Quarterly* 34.2 (2018): 99–114.

Jackson, Lucy C. M. M. *The Chorus of Drama in the Fourth Century BCE*. Oxford University Press, 2019.

Jeffers, Alison. 'Authority, Authorisation and Authorship: Participation in Community Plays in Belfast.' *Performance and Participation: Practices, Audiences, Politics*, edited by Anna Harpin and Helen Nicholson, Palgrave Macmillan, 2016, 209–229.

Kowalzig, Barbara. 'Changing Choral Worlds: Song-Dance and Society in Athens and Beyond.' *Music and the Muses: the Culture of Mousike in the Classical Athenian City*, edited by Penelope Murray and Peter Wilson, Oxford University Press, 2004, 39–66.

Marshall, C. W. '"Alcestis" and the Ancient Rehearsal Process (*P. Oxy.* 4546).' *Arion* 11.3 (2004): 27–45.

Matarasso, François. *A Restless Art: How Participation Won, and Why It Matters*. Calouste Gulbenkian, 2019.

Peponi, Anastasia-Erasmia. 'Theorizing the Chorus in Greece.' *Choruses, Ancient and Modern*, edited by Joshua Billings, et al., Oxford University Press, 2013, 15–34.

Sarra, Janis. 'An Opportune Moment: Retooling the Bankruptcy and Insolvency Act to Address Micro, Small and Medium Enterprise (MSME) Insolvency in Canada.' *Annual Review of Insolvency Law*, edited by Janis Sarra, Carswell, 2016, 119.

———. 'The Anthropocene in the Time of Trump: Financial Markets, Climate Change Risk and Economic Vulnerability.' *UBC Law Review*, 51.2 (2018), 489.

———. *From Ideas to Action: Governance Paths to Net Zero*. Oxford University Press, 2020.

Sarra, Janis, and Cheryl L. Wade. *Predatory Lending and the Destruction of the African-American Dream*. Cambridge University Press, 2020.

Scullion, Scott. '"Nothing to Do With Dionysus": Tragedy Misconceived as Ritual.' *Classical Quarterly* 52.1 (2002): 102–137.

Vernant, Jean-Pierre. *Myth and Society in Ancient Greece*. Zone Books, 1988.

Weiner, Albert B. 'The Function of the Tragic Greek Chorus.' *Theatre Journal* 32.2 (1980): 205–212.

Wiles, David. *Tragedy in Athens: Performance Space and Theatrical Meaning*. Cambridge University Press, 1997.

———. *A Short History of Western Performance Space*. Cambridge University Press, 2003.

7 Community Choruses and the Value of Participation in Contemporary Productions in the United Kingdom

Sarah Weston

Introduction

The community chorus is a contemporary trend in staging Greek tragedy in the United Kingdom. Comprised of an ensemble of non-professional, unpaid, local people supporting the professional actors in choral participation, productions using community choruses have taken place across the United Kingdom, tying choral recruitment to the theatre's participatory and community work. The chorus are not simply presented as non-professionals, but as a *community*, and accordingly as representatives of the city in which the production takes place, for example, described as a company of 'citizens' (Royal Lyceum Theatre and ATC). The community chorus is a social and theatrical practice, where values of civic participation, community arts, and theatrical vision are combined in the integration of community actors into a professional theatre process.

The purpose of this chapter is to discuss this convention through the lens of participation, focusing on the 'community' of community choruses. The choruses' aesthetics of unified song, speech, or movement as well as contemporary assumptions that the ancient chorus of Greek tragedy was inherently tied up with notions of democracy and citizenship can produce expectations that the chorus in itself is an act of community and civic participation (Laera 62). There is a danger therefore that the myths that assume idealist notions of democratic citizenship within the chorus of Greek tragedy could obfuscate the role and practice of the chorus in contemporary productions, generating an assumption that non-professional choral participation is inherently good. Through a discussion of the experiences of those who took part, I will assess the extent to which community participation is integrated within the contemporary staging of Greek tragedy, exploring what the participants felt they got out of being in a community chorus, and how their experiences contribute to understanding the role of the contemporary Greek chorus.

DOI: 10.4324/b22844-9

Methods

In this chapter I discuss three productions of Greek tragedies performed between 2015 and 2017 in the United Kingdom. My emphasis on participation means that the primary focus of this research is the words and responses of those who took part, rather than the intentions of the creative team, or a broader analysis of the production. Scholars such as Harrop and Eastman have discussed the use of the community chorus in contemporary productions, exploring its subversive role. Similarly, critics have questioned the draw of 'authenticity' in contemporary theatre practice surrounding non-professional participation in professional contexts (Holdsworth, Milling, and Nicholson 5). Building on this work, this chapter foregrounds the voices of those who took part, referring to three participant interviews, and a series of participant questionnaires across productions. I have chosen not to include details about the productions to protect those chorus members, and furthermore all the participant names are anonymised. However, it adds important context to clarify that the productions discussed took place at large, reputable regional theatres across the United Kingdom, were covered in the national press, and accordingly the scale of their reach situates them as prominent contemporary examples of the staging of Greek tragedy.

Defining Community Participation in the Chorus

What is meant by 'community' in the title 'community chorus'? Raymond Williams argues that community is a warm and persuasive term that has multiple meanings but is rarely meant as something negative (76). It is important then to scrutinise how the term is being employed in case the positive implications of the word mask something problematic. There are perhaps two ways in which community is meant in this choral staging convention. The first is a representative sense, where community refers to a specific existing community, such as one of location (the local area around the theatre for instance). The second is an economic sense, where community refers to those in the cast who do not perform for a living and want to take part in the production voluntarily (although some community chorus participants do perform for a living, or aspire to perform for living, alongside their volunteer status, which will be discussed later in the chapter). Accordingly, the 'community' of community chorus is a term that positions the chorus both in relation to a wider existing community, and as different from the professional cast. In recruiting a community chorus, the production team could desire to represent a community on stage, and/or they could desire a group of unpaid volunteers. In this sense, without a chorus having a connection to a broader community, it is difficult to define the 'community' of the community chorus as anything other than those in the production who *participate* rather than those who *work* (i.e., are paid).

Participatory theatre is a broad term that encompasses both professional and community practice, loosely encompassing the idea of those 'joining in' who would not normally take part in theatrical practice, particularly practice that is deemed professional, and it is perceived that there is some benefit or value to this joining in. Participating has been a clear trend of twenty-first-century theatre and performance practice in the United Kingdom, alongside a growth in theatre outreach and participation departments, where applied and community theatre work is developed alongside the professional work of a cultural institution. This means, as Harpin and Nicholson write, that questions of artistic labour are brought into dialogue with practices of participation (8), and furthermore that assumptions that participation is inherently for the social good must be re-evaluated.

The concept of active participation was a key principle of community arts in the twentieth century that aimed to disrupt the exclusive structures of traditional art. Through the principles of cultural democracy (that more people have access to creating culture, as opposed to the democratisation of culture, where 'high art' is more evenly distributed), the Community Arts Movement in Britain believed that access to the means of producing art, culture and creative forms would lead to greater engagement in society with further potential of wider social change (Jeffers, Introduction 1). Accordingly, taking part was a political imperative, with the idea that creative engagement led to greater representation, and more anti-hierarchical, democratic practice. Significantly, the political value of this is predicated on the community being involved in the creation and production of the art. This differs from some community-based practices, particularly that which has developed in the latter part of the twentieth century and into the twenty-first, where community participation is within already existing structures of an art institution, such as engaging with a play or exhibition. Jeffers encapsulates this in the shift in terminology from community arts to participatory arts. Here participatory arts means greater access for participants to art that already exists, whereas community arts is more aligned to the cultural democracy model of access to creative production ('Then and Now' 135). In this sense, I argue that the community chorus better fits the category of participatory rather than community arts, despite the use of the word community in the convention's labelling. Though the community are involved in creating the piece of art, the artwork for the most part already exists within the vision of the professional production team. Therefore, the community chorus convention, I believe, is an example of participatory theatre connected to a social motivation of increasing access to already existing, professional art.

Participation and the Chorus in Greek Tragedy

The community chorus is a reproduction of the convention of the Greek chorus, where a group of citizen-actors provided an extra voice of commentary to the protagonists of the play. Their performance comprised singing and dancing in unison; it has been described as a staging convention largely unfamiliar to contemporary Western audiences (Laera 66), and the traditional experience of chorality as something difficult for modern audiences or readers to grasp (Wiles; Zira). Though the ancient chorus may be unknowable to contemporary audiences, the adoption of the community chorus perhaps offers a glimpse at an implicit relationship between the chorus and civic society. Helen Eastman describes the contemporary community chorus as a cyclical return, renewing the idea of theatrical participation as a civic act, where the chorus is 'not just a reflection of what we mean by community, it is a participatory act defining community' (374).

However, critics have resisted easy attempts to equate the chorus to community building or democratic practice. Margherita Laera argues that the assumption of democracy and community within the structures of Greek tragedy is part of a construction within mainstream discourse of ancient Greece as the origin myth of Western culture (2). She argues that mythical narratives about 'classical' Greece are produced and reproduced through contemporary staging of Athenian drama, with productions operating as 'complex self-reflective rituals', drawing parallels between the present and past, and re-producing the utopic idea of drama as an embodiment of democracy (3). Building on this argument, Stephe Harrop highlights a danger in contemporary productions presenting the use of the community chorus in terms of community building, based on this nostalgic and utopic idea of Athenian drama as intrinsically connected to democracy (101). Accordingly, it cannot be assumed that the convention of the chorus offers a space for successful community building or democratic participation in the artistic process without further discussion of how participation is conceived and practised. Furthermore, there is a danger that the perception of Greek tragedy as a space for democratic participation can obscure the political and ethical questions that surround much participatory practice in the twenty-first century. As such, for both classical scholarship and participatory performance discourses, the convention of the community chorus offers an example of how the presumption of the inherent 'good' of participation or inherent 'good' of community can mask deeper complexities.

Community Building through Choral Participation

Participatory performance scholars in recent years have also resisted the idea that participation is automatically good. Harpin and Nicholson point out that the assumption that 'joining in' is inherently valuable needs to be re-evaluated in post-industrial society, as it cannot be assumed that to participate is an empowering act (3). Jen Harvie similarly argues that though non-professional participation can offer what seems like increased agency, this may in fact mean existing hierarchies within art production are simply masked (3). In the research I conducted, the community chorus participants broadly expressed a sense that participating was a positive experience, largely because of strong bonds of friendship that emerged in the process. The nature of the process, an intense rehearsal period with a clear goal, was significant to this sense of friendship and community, as one chorus member, Jessica, told me:

> Just knowing that you can meet a group of strangers or quite big group of strangers, and then six weeks, two months later, you can be living, breathing the same thing.

It was not just spending time together that engendered community feelings, but that participants spent time working together as a chorus, in Jessica's words, being 'merged into this sort of one, thinking, breathing, speaking set of people'. The majority of respondents agreed that participating led to strong bonds and friendship, a sense of pride and a sense of community.

However, some respondents problematised the value of the community in their production. For instance, Amalia discussed how the bonds between the chorus were diminished by how participation was conceived. In contrast to previous community projects in which she had participated, where the community had a strong input into the content and creative decisions of the show, Amalia described her experience in the Greek chorus as simply being told what to do and when. As creative decisions had been made prior to rehearsals she felt that she was simply learning pre-existing text and choreography. This made the experience uncollaborative and lacking in the kind of community-building she had felt in other projects. Following Harvie (2–3), Amalia felt her participation furthermore masked various ethical problems of how the community were treated. Because the value of participation was framed around the idea of recreating the citizen chorus there was perhaps a reliance on the chorus's historic function to serve as justification for the value of the community's participation. However, Amalia felt that further consideration of the community chorus' experience, as well as their creative input, was needed for it to be valuable. This problem was exacerbated by the production capitalising on the community, with the chorus as a key focus of the show's marketing, and the use of non-professional actors was mentioned in much of the positive press reaction. Accordingly, as the assumed purpose of the classical Greek chorus already embeds the concept of community within its structures, the use of this form could be a ready-made nod to a utopic ideal of community without much groundwork.

In this sense, community participation was a valuable activity for the production's reputation, but not necessarily for all those who participated. Specifically discussing community choruses, J. N. Benjamin writes how the convention sells the idea of community to both participants and audiences, where community is the word plastered on top of the production as a theatrical decision, rather than a process that the actors went through. Without an investment in a community-building process in the production, the concept of community remains a shallow nostalgia of an ancient political ideal that is perhaps symbolised in the production for an audience but is not necessarily experienced by the chorus.

Accordingly, community cannot be assumed as automatic in the experience of being in a community chorus. For some, the act of a shared goal, of working in unison, of speaking and moving together as one, inherently led to a sense of community and friendship that made the act of participation valuable. However, for others, this collaborative act was undermined by the lack of creative input and engagement in its conception, diminishing the quality of experience. In this alternative, the feeling of community bonding was not present when the participants did not feel represented creatively, and therefore the participatory process and building of a community felt secondary to the professional theatrical event.

The Professional Experience and the non-Professional, or Amateur

In his discussion of the passionate amateur (2013), Nicholas Ridout argues for the potential of theatre as a place where, within contemporary capitalism, one can experience something outside of the regular division of labour. He writes that the passionate amateurs of the theatre are those who 'work together for the production of value for one another ... in ways that refuse ... the division of labour that obtains under capitalism as usual' (15). While Ridout's discussion deliberately moves away from the fields of amateur, community, or participatory theatre, the idea that theatre is a place that resists binaries between work and non-work is particularly interesting in investigating those who choose to perform unpaid in a professional theatre production as part of their leisure time.

The amateur can interrupt their work with theatre, rather than doing theatre for work (Ridout 29). Yet, the notion of the amateur itself offers a contradiction: in one sense amateur is defined as doing something for the love of it, yet at the same time, it is also defined only in relation to what it is not, the professional. Nicholson, Holdsworth, and Milling suggest the idea of 'free time' to understand amateur labour, a concept that historically emerges out of the rise of industrial labour where leisure time becomes at risk of being valued through the terms of capital (160). This is particularly interesting in the case of theatre, where its live, ephemeral nature means the product of one's time might be something that cannot be captured (162). Moving through to contemporary patterns of work and leisure, Nicholson, Holdsworth, and Milling argue that the relationship between amateur and professional labour needs to be reassessed in the twenty-first century in terms of the blurring boundaries between work and leisure, the compression of space and time, and the erosion of stable working hours through the rise of precarious labour (163). It is worth noting that all three of these considerations perhaps are most notable for those working in the arts and cultural industries and can often be a barrier for those who want to work as a professional artist but are prevented by such precarity, unclear work/life balances, and unsociable hours. On one level, then, undertaking amateur labour may be an act of defiance against the hold that work has on one's time, an opportunity for the individual to make time for themselves despite their work. Yet, at the same time, unpaid participation could be the only option for those who cannot commit to a precarious career professionally (187–188).

One of the popular reasons given for joining the chorus was to experience a professional theatre production. This was an opportunity to perform on a large stage, in a reputable theatre in the local area, alongside professional actors and creative team. Learning how professional theatre productions come together was described as a meaningful experience by participants, as well as a sense of being inspired by the professional team and actors. This admiration of the process comes from a place of love, taking pleasure in discovering how theatre works for professionals. In this sense, regular divisions of labour felt dissolved, the community chorus experienced work as play, 'work that looks like it's not work', through their specific position of someone there for pleasure rather than necessity (Ridout 9).

Yet, the expectation to maintain professional production values while not being paid was problematic for some participants. This lack of pay is what designated the chorus as community, even if some of those in the chorus had professional theatre experience. Significantly, the status of being professional or not in many cases did not alter how performers were treated in the rehearsal process, nor how much of their time they gave up for the production. This for some created a tension between the demands of professional theatre and the value of participatory theatre processes. Gemma expressed some discomfort regarding the question of remuneration, even though her experience of being in the production had been broadly positive. In reflection, she wondered whether productions needed to do something about the lack of remuneration because of the amount of time that the chorus committed to the production. Gemma demonstrated how on two counts the chorus' participation felt more in line with expectations placed on those who are paid to perform: that the chorus gave up more of their time than the professionals, and that the chorus were set up as a commercial asset, through their use in the show's marketing.

This tension between professional and participatory attitudes was also present in how participants experienced the rehearsal process. Hannah discussed the difficulties of working with a professional director who treated the chorus the same as the professional actors, leaving her to feel out of her depth and stopping her from enjoying the experience as she was worried about 'letting the production down'. For Hannah, rather than equal treatment creating a sense of equality between the chorus and the professionals, it led to further division, as ignoring the important ways in which their performance experience was different left her feeling more exposed. Similarly, Amalia explained how the existing framework of her production, serving the script and choreography within the allotted rehearsal period, prevented some of the key experiences of community theatre processes, such as opportunity for reflection. In this sense, being treated like a professional was at the cost of some of the core values that might emerge from a community or amateur-driven process.

This is complicated further by unpacking the material cost of participation against a non-monetary value of participating. While some described the rehearsal process as intense, and a big commitment, others thrived on this and felt that putting this amount of time and commitment into the project made it more valuable during the performances. The challenge of achieving a professional standard of work alongside one's regular life of work or education, for some, was an important part of why they felt the experience valuable. As Jessica described:

> We didn't get a remuneration, we knew that it was purely voluntary. And I think that was enough for most of us, like the experience was so brilliant, we wouldn't have really wanted anything.

Similarly, Gemma, though expressing discomfort at the community not being paid, still felt in retrospect the overall experience was 'worth it' and her discomfort would not prevent her from participating again. However, she did state that her participation was only possible because at the time of the production she was in a stable place financially. In this sense, choral participation is also a matter of whether an individual can afford to give up this much of their free time, potentially excluding members because of financial insecurity.

Furthermore, for some committing large amounts of their free time was not 'worth it', with respondents feeling that the high level of commitment, rigour and intensity was not recompensed. Lucy described how the chorus had a longer rehearsal time than the professionals, but with 'no recognition either monetary or otherwise'. Additional to the time commitment, the level of responsibility and skill required from chorus members meant that their participation was professional in everything but name and financial renumeration. Amalia argued that the amount of hard work expected and the extent of the pressure placed on the chorus made the context of their participation professional, with that level of responsibility needing to be in some way remunerated. She felt that the artistic team's priority was that theatrical standards were high, meaning that a level of performance skill was needed in the community chorus. The chorus auditioned for their place, and she felt that anyone who did not meet a certain standard would not have been included, meaning that their participation was predicated on them possessing the skills needed for professional standard theatre. Many of the chorus members, according to her, were professional actors or aspiring professional actors and students. With participation premised on skill rather than to represent a specific community, the production's aim was to produce a professional standard production. Because of this, a significant amount of pressure was placed on the chorus that she felt had to be remunerated through pay as the chorus operated professionally in every aspect apart from receiving pay. Furthermore, without that sense of community representation, it is difficult to conceive of what made this chorus a 'community' other than the lack of pay.

If participation is professional in every sense but pay, is this community or professional participation? Following Ridout, if the non-professional engages in 'work that looks like it's not work', is it the nature of this engagement, or that they are not paid that makes it not look like work? This is a fundamental dilemma within the politics of using a community chorus: do the professional standards of the production expand the joy of doing something for the love of it, or does it undermine participatory pleasure through simply mirroring labour which is then unpaid? The convention of the community chorus within Greek drama typifies the political and ethical questions that emerge from bringing voluntary performers into a professional production. Like the presumption that the ancient chorus was an example of democracy in action (Laera 203), there is a danger that presuming greater community participation in contemporary cultural events leads to greater access, equality, and democracy in culture more widely.

Participation as Barter or Exchange

Fundamental to any practice that involves a combination of professionals and non-professionals is to question why theatre companies might invite non-professionals into an arts project, and why should non-professionals give up time for something they are not paid to do. It means a perpetual re-assessment of what we expect professionals to bring to a project, and what we expect non-professionals to bring. Matarasso argues that the professional artist brings skill and knowledge that arises from multiple experiences of practice and reflection, as well as resources, and a practical and embodied knowledge of other artistic work (91). In contrast, the non-professional may not have this expertise, but without this they can bring an open mind, questioning, and the freshness of a beginner's mind—they 'bring *need* to their work' (91–92, emphasis original). This concept of need is significant: it is this *need*, whether that be for a representative claim, for an act of love, or for the experience of professional theatre, that means the non-professional will give up their time without financial remuneration.

Baz Kershaw explores this dilemma when discussing the Ann Jellicoe model of community plays, where a professional production team works with a community cast to create a large-scale play about a moment in the local community's history. In response to criticism that this model encourages professional artists to use a local community for their own artistic ends, he argues that the relationship between the professionals and the community can be characterised by Eugenio Barba's term 'barter': the exchange of performance (193). In simple terms, one group may perform for another group and rather than exchange money for this performance, the receiving group performs something else in return. In Kershaw's re-conceiving of this idea for the community play, the professional company offer skill and craft in performance, and in exchange the community group offer local and authentic understanding of the place in which the play is taking place. Kershaw states that whether this barter leads to equality between the community and the professionals depends on the specific case in point and is not automatic within the process. Perhaps in the community chorus, an altered barter process takes place. The professional team bring expertise and the opportunity to take part in a professional production. In return, the chorus provide their time, skill, commitment, and in some cases, their own creativity, thoughts, and passions. The community chorus bring need, whether this is a need to perform for the love of it, a need to meet other like-minded people and socialise, or a need to experience a professional production.

To further understand the concept of barter in relation to the community chorus I will contrast the experiences of two participants, Jessica and Amalia. Firstly, Jessica described the experience as enriching and something she would love to do again. In her case, the professional values applied in the rehearsal and production process accelerated the feelings of community and friendship found in the chorus. In this barter, professional standards in exchange for her time, commitment, and passion synthesised in a sense of community bonding and an event that everyone involved in could be proud of. In this production, most of the chorus, in her words, were novices to the stage. But, by the end of the process, she argues they achieved a sense of equality with the professionals—what she described as 'one big family'. Something unique was created in the coming together of professional and non-professional artists that could not have been achieved in another way, as this uniqueness arose precisely out of the sharing of different assets (Matarasso 93).

In contrast, Amalia spoke of the experience as bordering on exploitative. In her case, a sense of community was lacking as the production focused much more on creating a polished performance than on the experiences of the chorus. She felt that she was only there because her performance skills were 'good enough', and whether she got something out of the experience seemed secondary. In this case, the process of barter is absent. Professional skill from the production team was exchanged for a professional standard of skill from the chorus. Rather than a process of barter, the production asked for standards of performance that would normally be paid, instead of the process of exchanging different competencies. The non-professionals were expected to relate to the art as a job, rather than as exploration of other needs (Matarasso 92). Instead of, in Kershaw's words, barter as a process towards equality (193), equal standards were expected from the beginning, preventing a participatory process where other values could emerge, or other needs be met. Without the emergence of these non-monetary values, Amalia felt that she had given time, commitment, and skill with no recompense, financial or otherwise. This was further exacerbated by the large number of trained performers in this production participating for professional experience to help their career development. In their case, the need gained from community participation is connected to the need of any professional actor: the need for pay in exchange for work, rather than a need of the non-professional, connected to personal, social, and cultural needs.

Conclusion

In a promotional video for The Lyceum and ATC's production of *The Suppliant Women*, the production team position their work as harking back to the classical Greek way of making and performing theatre. Greek tragedy is presented as a form of theatre which is connected to democracy and community dialogue, where 'you have a city talking to itself' (Lyceum Theatre). While there is much to be applauded in the desire to connect a major regional theatre back to the citizens, there is a danger in lifting an ancient performance convention into a contemporary setting in the hope of recreating a nostalgic conception of community or democracy. Following Laera, the origin myth that equates drama and democracy in the Greek context can make false equivalences between our world and a world that operated in a completely different political, social, and economic system, and furthermore is largely conceived of in contemporary Western thinking in an idealised, nostalgic way (3). Community participation in Greek tragedy requires consideration of ethical and political debates beyond the recreation of ancient conventions, with practitioners also considering key contemporary questions of participatory performance. For example, if a production only requires the performance skills of a community, then perhaps a reconsideration is needed as to whether this is really a voluntary participatory project. Practitioners wishing to invite community participation into a professional production must consider on what basis the community feels compelled to join in, and whether the process allows for genuine exchange, based on community need.

This chapter has aimed to highlight some of the challenges of involving community participants in a professional production, particularly with Greek tragedy where the assumption of the inherent relationship between the ancient chorus, community and democracy could mask problematic practice. Framing this within the debates of cultural democracy, the convention of the community chorus does not automatically lead to community dialogue, despite its historic function. Rather it is a space for community members to take part in professional practice, with the potential to create a joyous, memorable, or significant experience for those individuals, leading to long-lasting friendships. It is clear that the community chorus can be an enriching experience, and as important as it is not to assume that the convention is inherently community-based or democratic, it is also important not to assume that it is inherently exploitative because it involves voluntary labour. I believe from this research that there is a non-monetary worth in community participation, and many participants knowingly join a project with no desire for remuneration, with participation as an act to temporarily escape the relationship between time, labour and pay. However, two things must be considered. Firstly, the replication of an ancient convention does not automatically replicate the convention's social function or value. Secondly, by instead framing participation within our contemporary structures, practitioners must ensure that the exchange of participants' time is fairly met, ensuring that participation is 'worth it'.

Works Cited

Benjamin, J. N. 'Are Community Choruses Exploitative?' *Exeunt*, 25 Feb. 2019, www.exeuntmagazine.com/features/community-choruses-exploitative. Accessed 20 Aug. 2022.

Eastman, Helen. 'Chorus in Contemporary British Theatre.' *Choruses, Ancient and Modern*, edited by Joshua Billings, Felix Budelmann and Fiona Macintosh, Oxford University Press, 2013, 363–376.

Harpin, Anna, and Helen Nicholson. 'Performance and Participation.' *Performance and Participation: Practices, Audiences, Politics*, edited by Anna Harpin and Helen Nicholson, Palgrave, 2017, 1–15.

Harrop, Stephe. 'Greek Tragedy, Agonistic Space, and Contemporary Performance.' *New Theatre Quarterly* 34.2 (2018): 99–114.

Harvie, Jen. *Fair Play—Art, Performance and Neoliberalism*. Palgrave Macmillan, 2013.

Holdsworth, Nadine, Jane Milling, and Helen Nicholson. 'Theatre, Performance, and the Amateur Turn.' *Contemporary Theatre Review* 27.1 (2017): 4–17.

Jeffers, Alison. 'Introduction.' *Culture, Democracy and the Right to Make Art: The British Community Arts Movement*, edited by Alison Jeffers and Gerri Moriarty, Bloomsbury, 2017, 1–34.

———. 'Then and Now: Reflections on the Influence of the Community Arts Movement on Contemporary Community and Participatory Arts.' *Culture, Democracy and the Right to Make Art: The British Community Arts Movement*, edited by Alison Jeffers, and Gerri Moriarty, Bloomsbury, 2017, 133–160.

Kershaw, Baz. *The Politics of Performance: Radical Theatre as Cultural Intervention*. Routledge, 1992.

Laera, Margherita. *Reaching Athens: Community, Democracy and Other Mythologies in Adaptations of Greek Tragedy*. Peter Lang, 2013.

Lyceum Theatre. 'The Making of *The Suppliant Women*'. *YouTube*, 29 Sep. 2016. www.youtube.com/watch?v=Pj_qYUeYU2A. Accessed 31 Mar. 2023.

Matarasso, F. *A Restless Art: How Participation Won, and Why It Matters*. London: Calouste Gulbenkian Foundation, 2019.

Nicholson, Helen, Nadine Holdsworth, and Jane Milling. *The Ecologies of Amateur Theatre*. Palgrave Macmillan, 2018.

Ridout, Nicholas. *Passionate Amateurs: Theatre, Communism and Love*. University of Michigan Press, 2013.

Royal Lyceum Theatre and ATC. 'Press Release for *The Suppliant Women*, by Aeschylus. Royal Lyceum Theatre, Edinburgh.' *Royal Lyceum Theatre*, 2015.

Wiles, David. *Greek Theatre Performance: An Introduction*. Cambridge University Press, 2000.

Williams, Raymond. *Keywords: A Vocabulary of Culture and Society*. 2nd ed. Fourth Estate, 1988.

Zira, Magdalena. *The Problem of the Chorus in Contemporary Revivals of Greek Tragedy and Directorial Solutions in the Last Forty Years*, Ph.D. Dissertation. King's College London, 2019.

Part III
Academics and/as Practitioners

8 Sheffest

Bringing Ancient Greek Theatre to Sheffield

Lottie Parkyn

Is there a doctor ... some don from Queen's
who can tell the rest of us what all this means.

(Harrison 97)

The poet and playwright Tony Harrison once sarcastically noted in his play *The Trackers of Oxyrhynchus* that ancient Greek—and subsequently its theatre—was a subject only understood by the academically enlightened and not the everyman. As a working-class male, who had only received a classical education due to the 1944 Education Act and the establishment of grammar schooling, Harrison was acutely aware of the politics of accessibility in Classics.[1] Harrison's perspective, demonstrated in his play, was that access to this knowledge was tied to a class structure where the elite controlled what engagement the rest of society could have. While a number of individuals and projects have sought to break down these barriers so that the subject matter of Classics can be enjoyed by all, it is notable that the academy's interest in outreach and widening participation developed significantly in the 2010s. The Sheffield Festival of Ancient Drama (Sheffest) hosted in June 2012 was one such project, curated by me and a colleague, Matthew Shipton, with the ambitious goal of exposing a community to the theatre of the ancient Greeks through a four-day festival.

At the time of the festival, we were unsure of how to evaluate our impact, and even now in retrospect it is difficult to know how to measure success. Our mission was to create an inclusive event for the city of Sheffield; however, in our naivety, we struggled to find the right balance. In some ways we, as relative outsiders to the city, thrust ancient Greek theatre upon the local community and evangelised about the benefits without knowing if there really was a broad appetite for engaging with this. Steven Hadley describes this as 'democratising culture', which approaches widening participation in cultural activities 'on the basis of received ideas of both the definition and value of culture' by institutions; in this case, various constituents of the Classics ecology (Hadley 9). There is often the belief that there is a reluctance

DOI: 10.4324/b22844-11

by a community to engage with what the institutions deem as the 'official' culture and by offering opportunities to engage it would do the participants some good. This is very different to the notion of 'cultural democracy', where communities and individuals themselves 'have substantive social freedom to make versions of culture' and are supported in these endeavours (Wilson, Gross, and Bull 3). I believe our intention was to fall somewhere between the two concepts; however, I am now convinced that we were unconsciously leaning towards the former.

We struggled to impact significantly outside a group that I have labelled as the 'classically enthused', although there was support and enthusiasm from a number of local cultural groups. I now ask myself if we accidentally perpetuated the kind of Classics Harrison was skewering. In the spirit of such reflection, this chapter will use Sheffest as a case study to discuss and address questions around outreach in the Classics ecology. While there is a passionate desire to impart knowledge conserved in the ecology, I ask whether this can, at times, be misguided. Rather than parachuting ourselves into the area with a prepared vision, could we have provided knowledge and support so that Sheffielders could devise their own creative work around Greek tragedy as outlined in the notion of cultural democracy? Is there a disconnect between the perception of the value of classical knowledge and what this value means to those outside this ecology? Do some constituents in the Classics ecology naively expect that once outsiders have some engagement with the ancient world, that they will then place the same level of value on the subject?

The Motivation of the 'Classically Enthused'

The 'classically enthused' by my definition are people and organisations already committed to the framing of the knowledge of ancient Greece and Rome as 'Classics' and who perhaps have some connection the discipline. This would include, but is not limited to, academics, teachers at primary and secondary schools, and individuals representing cultural institutions, including theatre practitioners. This cohort will have had some exposure to a classical education or will have engaged with the ancient world within their work, and place value on access to the subject. This value can be problematic as the ancient Greeks and Romans are often put into the mythical context of being the origins of 'Western' society; doing this enforces the exclusionary notion of Western superiority, as the introduction to this volume discusses. The organising team (including myself), as well as a variety of other parties we engaged with while creating Sheffest, certainly fell into the category of the 'classically enthused'.

Academia

Matthew Shipton, who at the time was a fellow Classics PhD student and originally from Sheffield, approached me with the idea of creating a festival of ancient drama that took advantage of a new theatre site above the South Yorkshire city's main train station. Sheffield itself provides many nods to the ancient cities of Athens and Rome.[2] In 2011, as part of a regeneration project of the area surrounding Sheffield train station, a theatre, described by the city council as an amphitheatre, was opened in a location overlooking the city, similar to how the Theatre of Dionysus uses Athens as its impressive backdrop.[3]

Shipton and I are both passionate about improving access to the ancient world—the new Sheffield theatre therefore felt to us like an opportunity for exactly this kind of access work. We both came from what would historically have been considered unconventional classical education backgrounds. Neither of us had attended private schools or were well versed in Latin or ancient Greek; however, we were fascinated by what the drama of the ancient Athenians could communicate to contemporary society and had embarked on doctorates with Edith Hall alongside full-time employment.[4] We were convinced of the value that having access to at least some classical education has, and our backgrounds reinforced the notion that we should share this knowledge with those who did not normally have access to it. Perhaps if our classical education journey had been more conventional, our attitude to widening participation in the field may have been different.

We were certainly working within, and influenced heavily by, the Classics ecology. Alongside our doctoral work, we had been enrolled on to a two-year public engagement course run by the Archive of Performances of Greek and Roman Drama (APGRD) entitled *Communicating Ancient Greece and Rome* (CAGR) in the autumn of 2010.[5] Here we were introduced to like-minded students and were encouraged to brainstorm potential outreach activities or projects that would share our expertise with audiences outside of the field. From this course, more members of the Sheffest team were recruited who held similar views to myself and Shipton concerning widening participation.[6] As a group we were the epitome of the 'classically enthused'.

In the early 2010s, public engagement was a relatively new area in academia. All subjects, but particularly the humanities, needed to prove themselves as a viable sector within Higher Education. Subject fields had to demonstrate that they were worth investment from the coalition government that was in power in this period, as well as from their own universities who were increasingly needing to act as businesses rather than, it seemed, supporting the desire to uncover new ideas through research.[7] There was a shift from providing a wide-ranging education for all to a need to, in a data-driven manner, indicate how much research and tertiary education was contributing to the British economy. In an environment where science, technology, and business-related studies could easily prove their real-world application, demonstrating their financial benefits to both academic institutions and politicians, humanities subjects such as the study of philosophy, democracy, and the arts of the ancient past struggled. Classics and Ancient History departments were being threatened with restructuring or closure.[8]

To compound this anxiety, the first Research Excellence Framework (REF) evaluation was on the horizon, and one of the key aims was to measure research impact which in turn would 'provide a basis for distributing funding primarily by reference to research excellence, and to fund excellent research in all its forms wherever it is found' (Eastwood).[9] Academics, particularly those in the humanities, were critical of this new assessment, asserting that impact can be hard to assess over only a few years and in a manner that would be regarded as fair or as impartial (Shepherd). Public engagement and outreach activities were one way an academic or department could demonstrate the significance or impact that their subject had for a wider external community. However, these terms were often used with a variety of meanings, prompting confusion within the academic community about their definition and whether they constitute impact.[10] An additional benefit of communicating research in this manner was the potential to encourage future students to take on these subjects, boosting enrolment numbers on university courses which often correlated with how much money each department had to spend or whether they could continue to function. This need to prove relevance certainly influenced, consciously or subconsciously, the majority of those working within the Classics ecology at the time, particularly in academia, prompting courses such as CAGR and the rise in public engagement projects in the early 2010s.

School Outreach

The engagement of future generations and increasing exposure to the theatre of the ancient Athenians was particularly at the forefront of our minds when Shipton and I started to flesh out the foundations of Sheffest. The festival would run for four days with fringe activities taking place around the main event, a newly translated version of Aeschylus' *Prometheus Bound* by Henry Stead, renamed *Prometheus Chained* in homage to Sheffield's industrial past. Outside of the main production, our other activities manifested as a series of talks and short performances which offered the people of Sheffield a taster of the classical world, while an afternoon of workshops was scheduled specifically for local comprehensive schoolchildren who were either studying Classical Civilisation, Drama, or English at Key Stage 4 (GCSE level).

A general interest in Greek mythology and subjects concerning the ancient world were seeing a resurgence thanks to the popularity of the *Percy Jackson* and *Harry Potter* franchises. However, apart from the brief exploration of the Greeks and Romans that took place as part of the Key Stage 1 national curriculum, the majority of children who were educated in the comprehensive system would have little opportunity to directly engage with this subject in subsequent schooling in comparison to their privately educated counterparts who had more access to subjects such as Latin, Greek, and Ancient History (Hunt and Holmes-Henderson). Interestingly, comprehensive students could briefly engage with these topics in isolated occurrences that were potentially divorced from their ancient context, such as through studying Sophocles' *Antigone* which appeared on the A-Level theatre studies set text list.[11] In 2012, a number of educational theatre companies, such as Actors of Dionysus, and ancient history inspired programmes, such as The Iris Project, had already been operating for a while; however, the feedback we received from teachers working in Sheffield was that bringing well-known companies into northern state-funded schools could be hard to justify financially.[12] There was a desire to expose students to live performances of Greek drama; however, when productions of ancient Greek theatre were staged in the United Kingdom, they were often performed in London, and rarely appeared on tour in Sheffield.[13]

We approached a number of schools through local contacts, and approximately 100 children attended our afternoon workshop. While obtaining this number of attendees was a success in our eyes, in retrospect we neglected to follow up either through conducting an immediate survey following the workshop or a few years later to see what impact this left upon the students. Impact data can be hard to analyse, as emphasised in the REF2014 report which stated that 'those who are impacted are frequently themselves unable to describe, let alone quantify, the effects' (65). Did this workshop inspire them to pursue Classics or theatre in the future, or leave them with a love of Greek drama? We do not know. Certainly, the experience of engaging with new subject matter within school outreach is very different from that of general public outreach. Whereas a number of deciding factors and choices play a part in what inspires someone to buy a ticket to a festival and engage, with a student workshop the individuals have relatively little choice about their involvement. They can passively take part, though to a certain extent, they are still engaged due to the expected and mandatory nature of class activities. Equally, the children that attended were students of proactive teachers who could be described as already 'classically enthused'. Most teachers had studied the Greeks and Romans at some point during their education or were already fans of classical storytelling and mythology. We were not, therefore, reaching an audience of teachers and students outside the Classics ecology.

Funding and Support from within the Classics Ecology

In hindsight it is clear that in some ways we were working within an ecology that was already supportive of the classical world and we found it easy to recruit those who were equally a part of this mindset. When looking for financial support, the festival was funded by the already classically converted. Small amounts of support came from organisations such as the Classical Association, the Gilbert Murray Trust, the Society for the Promotion of Hellenic Studies (SPHS), the APGRD, and the classically focused theatre production company, Omniprop Productions. Each group were already supporters of making the classical world accessible to all and therefore, in some ways, our initial work took place in a vacuum. We did not need to convince them of the value that staging a festival like this would have and members of the Sheffest team had connections to these funding bodies.[14] Additionally, a few years previously, the Iris Project had hosted a festival of Classics in London, which laid the groundwork for outreach projects such as Sheffest.[15]

The intention was to have a sense of local community at the heart of this play. In terms of staging, this was reflected in the cast and playwright/directorial choices; however, the final demographic of the audience did not fully reflect this in the way we imagined. Despite prolific marketing in Sheffield and the surrounding areas, we discovered a significant portion of the audience was made up of those we would consider as part of the 'classically enthused'. Groups of academics and students travelled from Oxford and London to attend the festival. While we were (and still are) grateful for the support, we would have liked to have seen greater representation from Greek tragedy first-timers. The low attendance from this demographic was perhaps due to a number of factors, such as the weather being unfavourable and more established festivals taking place in the city at the same time, however fundamentally it would appear that the community of Sheffield were not convinced of the value—or the 'culturally enthused' definition of value—of Greek tragedy enough to engage.

Sheffest certainly was a product of the Classics ecology, and it is interesting to note that even as we tried to engage external groups, we were operating mostly within that ecology. But this needs to be contextualised in the very real sense of threat to our discipline we felt at the time: our urgent articulations of the value of engaging with the ancient Greek and Roman worlds came from the perception of this threat across overlapping networks, including the community of Edith Hall's PhD students, the APGRD, and particular funders (who were not unknown to us). It is no accident that these same networks had previously been galvanised to defend the value of Classics following the attempted cuts at Royal Holloway (see Note 8). We were all connected and shared the view that intrinsically there was value in the knowledge of the ancient world; this view was sharpened in the face of those who seemed to be saying that there was no value in it at all. Our attempts to share this knowledge with others were made in good faith, but on reflection, we needed to do more to persuade those outside of our immediate ecology—organisations, funders, the local community—that there were reasons to value ancient Greek theatre today and so support our project.

Outsiders in the Classics Ecology

For the purposes of this chapter, I consider 'outsiders' as those external to the bubble that the 'classically enthused' inhabit; they often are individuals, communities, and institutions that the Classics ecology attempts to impress the relevance and, most importantly, the value of their field upon with various levels of success. They do not necessarily lack insight into the subject: the worth of knowledge concerning the classical world may be understood in part, however, this group do not have the same level of motivation that the 'classically enthused' have, which can hinder the progress of outreach projects. Outlying factors, such as their own ability to support projects financially or with their time, or that classical outreach is one of many cultural activities among already established programming, can also contribute to making decisions on what is seen as valuable to a community. In regard to Sheffest, this cohort contained a number of organisations and people at the local as well as the national level.

The Hurdles of Gaining Support from Outsiders

While we assembled a core team, mainly of PhD students who were enrolled in the CAGR program, all of whom had their own individual creative strengths, Shipton and I knew it would be crucial to obtain as much support from Sheffield, and those outside of the Classics ecology, as possible. A shortlist of Sheffield-based agencies to approach was created including Sheffield City Council, Sheffield Theatres, Creative Sheffield and Sheffield International Venues. We expected that through these partnerships, opportunities could be identified and therefore the festival could take on a distinctly local character, reflecting Sheffield values of creativity and innovation, inclusivity and rootedness. We had hoped by collaborating with these groups we could gain access to their already established local audiences through their endorsement, gain guidance on how best to work with the communities of Sheffield, and, of course, funding support would be welcomed.

Our first stop was investigating the potential for a partnership with, or support from, Sheffield's best-known theatre, The Crucible, particularly as the headlining event of our festival would be an open-air performance of a Greek tragedy. The Crucible has had very little to do with ancient Greek theatre ever since its establishment, which was surprising given that Greek tragedy may have inspired the design of the stage (Billington).[16] Like the National Theatre in London, The Crucible had championed new work alongside canonical plays such as productions of Shakespeare; however, the National Theatre also regularly embraced ancient Greek theatre in their scheduling. In the 2000s and early 2010s, artistic director Nicholas Hytner championed the genre and commissioned multiple tragedies by well-established directors such as Peter Hall and newer artists like Katie Mitchell; Polly Findlay's production of *Antigone* opened shortly before Sheffest. Hytner was, and still is, very much a member of the 'classically enthused', which is emphasised by his privileged educational background: he attended Manchester Grammar School where a classical education was certainly provided, followed by a degree in English from Cambridge University, where engagement with 'classical' literature would have taken place (Rokison-Woodall). In contrast, Daniel Evans, who in 2010 took on the role of artistic director of Sheffield Theatres—which includes The Crucible—was not 'in' the Classics ecology in the same way as

Hytner, attending a Welsh-speaking comprehensive school near Pontypridd, South Wales, before going straight into training at Guildhall School of Music and Drama. This is perhaps reflected in his programming choices, which opted for more recent canonical texts and musicals.

Shipton and I met with members of Sheffield Theatres leadership team to discuss our project with the view to obtaining support. While it was not explicitly said, it was implied that The Crucible wanted to stage plays that would strategically engage and excite their audiences, and the tragedies of the Greeks did not currently seem to fit this vision. This surprised us at the time, as we, as part of the 'classically enthused', could not understand why those outside of our ecology, but yet from an often-overlapping ecology such as the world of theatre, did not place the same amount of value on these productions as we did. Perhaps there was a perception that a Sheffield audience would reject Greek tragedy due to the lack of engagement with classical knowledge within the community, in a similar manner to those who struggle to engage with Shakespeare and subsequently avoid related productions. Sheffield Theatres were committed to making theatre accessible and had already agreed to collaborate with the Sheffield Universities to stage the first International Student Drama Festival around our planned dates (Stone), which stretched their resources that were already under pressure. This meant that they were unable to financially assist our endeavour nor provide any logistical aid as payment in kind, which was a common response when potential local funders were approached.

The UK coalition government of Conservatives and Liberal Democrats that had formed in 2010 and the austerity program that was implemented following this deeply impacted the resources available in many communities around the United Kingdom, particularly in regard to arts and education provision, and Sheffield was no exception. In fact, Nick Clegg, the deputy Prime Minister and Liberal Democrat leader, had represented the Sheffield Hallam constituency, and a sense of disillusionment and betrayal by their MP was prevalent when speaking to locals: in their view, he was complicit in making the decisions that were directly impacting their community. This inspired the choice of a steampunk-styled production of Aeschylus' *Prometheus Bound* that drew upon the history and industrial background of Sheffield, but that also leaned into this frustration within the community. Justifying this decision in an article ahead of the festival, Shipton claimed '*Prometheus* was firmly in mind ... the conflict around coalitions, the establishment of a new regime and reaction to a new social and political environment has been a backdrop for the last few years' ('Why Prometheus?'). However, our use of this myth was also intended as a story of new beginnings and hope. Sheffield Council, in collaboration with housing company Urban Splash, had, prior to the introduction of the austerity program, commissioned the building of the theatre space in an area that was seeing great regeneration. Sheaf Valley Park had been made up of blocks of dilapidated council flats and had been earmarked for redevelopment. Between the buildings on the top of the valley and the railway station below, pockets of previously unkempt land were transformed into eight hectares of open space for residents to use. But by the time the theatre had been completed, the local council had faced financial cuts which left them with very little ability to support community projects in the new space.[17] Despite this our contacts at the council were enthusiastic about our project, and contributed in the ways they could, such as offering free rental of event fencing and guidance on health and safety measures. Simon Parker, Director of New Local Government Network, described this style of support that was taking place in various areas around the country as local authorities 'moving from a position where they handed out grants to one where they support the cultural sector to find premises, access funding and tap into the energy of local residents' (Harvey 5).

Without concrete financial support from the local government, we sought funding from national organisations such as Arts Council England, though without success. This was not surprising. The economic pressures that were seen in Sheffield were replicated at the national level. The Culture, Media and Sport Committee delivered a report on the funding of the arts and heritage on 22 March 2011 that outlined a cut in Arts Council budgets by £23 million ('Funding of the Arts', Section 2.19). In addition, 2012 saw the culmination of the four-year Cultural Olympiad festival which had been created to build up to and run alongside the London 2012 Olympic Games.[18] This was a hugely ambitious nationwide program in which arts and cultural activities were made accessible to the public. Funding had been provided by Arts Council England, Legacy Trust UK, and the Olympic Lottery Distributor, and in speaking to related representatives our project fitted the criteria for support, especially as there had been a desire to tie in the modern Olympic games with their ancient Greek past. However, the funding deadlines had closed prior to the conception of our festival. Despite this, Sheffield Council were happy to acknowledge our series of events as part of the Cultural Olympiad activities, particularly as it had a strong local community focus, and publicised our festival alongside the multitude of other events taking place in Sheffield. Unable to secure financing through local organisations or national funders, the festival was reliant on the aforementioned support from 'classically enthused' groups predominantly based in southeast England.

The Local Community

David Wiles describes Greek tragedy as 'a device which allowed the Athenians to come together and collectively think through their problems ... and its performance was part of what turned a collection of men into a polis' (48). With Sheffest, particularly in regard to the performance of *Prometheus Chained*, our intention was to bring the people of Sheffield together in a similar manner and give the polis—the city—an opportunity to contemplate and question current affairs. The involvement of Sheffield community members was an important part of casting the production. It would have been easier to have worked with actors from Oxford and London who we already knew and who could rehearse at locations and times more convenient for the production team; however, we felt it was vital that we had a cast representative of the area for a number of reasons. The presence of the new theatre and its classical connotations had been central to the development of the festival, and thus presented the opportunity to continue to evoke the style of the ancient Athenians by making this a community event, as it would have been in fifth-century Athens. By having a cast whose accents mirrored those of the local audience, it was our belief that this could soothe any concerns of being unable to engage with the classical subject matter as the audience would see themselves represented on stage. Contemporary directors had already taken similar approaches when dealing with tragedy. Claudia Bosse had staged *Die Perser* (Aeschylus' *Persians*) in Geneva, Vienna, and Brunswick (2006–2008), where the chorus comprised up to 500 locals. Bryan Doerries, the artistic director of Theater of War Productions, has also followed this trend in staging his dramatic readings of Greek tragedy (and other plays), most notably in his *Antigone in Ferguson* project (2016) in which the chorus performs as a choir composed of activists, young people, teachers, police officers, and concerned citizens from a number of communities.

Reminiscent of how Peter Hall and Tony Harrison utilised the Yorkshire accent during their production of *The Oresteia* at the National Theatre in 1981, our team made the stylistic choice to lean into the local accent.[19] We had already tested using the Sheffield accent at a showcase during the infancy of the project where we gave a small Sheffield audience the first look at our plans for the festival's central production. We thought that by hearing the language in the audience's own local dialect, the common preconception that ancient Greek theatre is an elitist genre for those who speak with a Received Pronunciation accent would subside. By utilising Sheffielders, we believed that we were attempting to break away from the already 'classically enthused'. Our final cast was made up of mainly local amateur actors, only some of whom had an awareness of ancient Greek drama. The majority auditioned out of a love for theatre and the chance to be part of a new project that featured their home city.

We saw this draw of engaging with the city emerge in most aspects of our outreach. For those who were from Sheffield, whether they were a part of the cast, an audience member, a member of the council, or a student, it certainly seemed that the city was a main attraction of the festival, rather than the opportunity to experience ancient Greek theatre. We did see attendance from the various local connections we made during the early days of promoting Sheffest, and the cast brought in friends and family who had never seen Greek drama performed in the open air. However, a big influence in deciding to buy a ticket for *Prometheus Chained* was certainly the location—we were one of the first groups to use the hilltop theatre—and the promise of Sheffield-inspired staging. After seeing one choral ode during the workshop, a student remarked that she felt more connected to the history of the city than ever before, an endorsement that we had made an impact on at least one Sheffield resident, though perhaps not the impact we were expecting. In hindsight, it seems that we tied the play and the festival so closely to the city that perhaps the value of ancient Greek theatre that we intended to impress became a secondary thought to the communities we were hoping to engage with: in fact, it was a conduit to bringing them closer to their home.

Lessons Learned

There appears to be a large disconnect between the value that the 'classically enthused' place on the subject of ancient Greece and Rome, and the value that outsiders see it has (or does not have). Proponents of the subject within the Classics ecology often fail to understand this. As Hadley notes about those who attempt to democratise culture, they assume there is a reluctance to engage with the topic and that they can 'do some good' by creating outreach projects (9). Assumptions around value mean that outreach projects generated within the Classics ecology often fall into this mindset. Certainly, my interaction with those in Sheffield should have involved more listening to identify whether this festival was truly wanted or needed by those outside of the 'classically enthused'.

While we wanted to widen participation, we were unable to fully realise this idea for financial reasons and had to charge for tickets. This immediately placed a barrier between those who might be interested but could not afford or were reluctant to pay for an experience they were unsure about, and those who could afford or were willing to pay based upon the 'value' they understood ancient Greek theatre to have. It should not have been surprising that the 'classically enthused' were more open to purchasing a ticket than those who did not assume the inherent value of a relatively obscure Greek tragedy. With our production, we thought we were disrupting the closedness of the Classics ecology; however, perhaps the theatre—and its cost—reinforced a sense of elitism and closedness.

Of course, we could not completely control who watched this open-air production. A group of youngsters who were riding their bikes past the venue that evening watched the majority of *Prometheus Chained* from a distance without having a ticket. Their interest was piqued in an uncontrolled way, and perhaps this can inform our future thoughts on engaging with those outside of the Classics ecology. In line with discussions about cultural democracy versus democratising culture, allowing individuals to make their own decisions on how to engage with ancient Greece and Rome and then finding ways to creatively support that engagement rather than preaching of the values of the classical world may be a more productive way forward.

Notes

1. See Parkyn 117–124 and Hall, *Tony Harrison* 16.
2. George Orwell claimed that the town was built on seven hills, like Rome, and Sheffield Town Hall, the civic centre, is proudly adorned with a statue of the metalworking god, Vulcan, paying homage to the city's international reputation for industrial activity, particularly in steel making.
3. For more information about the 'amphitheatre', see: www.bbc.co.uk/news/uk-england-south-yorkshire-14950920 (accessed 19 Aug. 2023).
4. I attended a comprehensive school that saw value in teaching Classical Civilisation which subsequently put me on a pathway to study the subject at the University of Birmingham; Shipton engaged with 'Classics' through an MA at the Open University.
5. For more information on this programme, see: www.apgrd.ox.ac.uk/about-us/programmes/communicating-ancient-greece-and-rome (accessed 19 Aug. 2023).
6. Including Henry Stead (Open University) who translated and adapted *Prometheus Chained*, Helen Slaney (Oxford) who directed the production, and Jarrid Looney (Royal Holloway) who oversaw our education outreach.
7. See Shepperd as well as Sayer.
8. A number of the Sheffest production team also had been a part of the successful 'Save Classics' campaign that was started when Royal Holloway, University of London had threatened cuts to its Classics department in 2011 (on the campaign, see Bullen). In the summer of 2012, just prior to Sheffest taking place, it was announced that the University of Birmingham had also earmarked their Institute of Archaeology and Antiquity for closure. Edith Hall wrote in her blog about the comparisons between our production of *Prometheus Chained* at the festival and the 'crisis' that British Higher Education was facing ('The Promethean Politics of Education').
9. REF was established to evaluate the research impact of British Higher Education Institutions. It was first used in 2014 to assess the period 2008–2013.
10. For work on defining terms such as public engagement, outreach, and impact, see Bridges 2–3 and Duncan, Manners, and Miller 3. Bridges goes on to claim that confusion of these terms still exists in Classics (5).
11. See further this volume's introduction (5–6).
12. For more on the activities of The Iris Project, see: http://irisproject.org.uk (accessed 19 Aug. 2023). In recent years, Actors of Dionysus have set up a free workshop campaign (Rogers). On aod, see also Bullen, this volume.
13. National Theatre Live would be shown around the country in cinemas and other locations to improve accessibility to theatre, but it was still in its infancy at this point, with the first broadcast in 2010. The Actors of Dionysus were an exception and performed at The Crucible between the years of 2000–2003.
14. For example, SPHS had previously sponsored a series of community theatre workshops I ran in Birmingham around Euripides' *Electra*, and Helen Slaney, our director, had worked with Omniprop Productions in the past.
15. See: http://irisproject.org.uk/index.php/the-iris-project/projects/ancient-theatre/12-iris-festival-of-classics (accessed 19 Aug. 2023).
16. Between 1999 and 2003, the theatre hosted a handful of external groups performing tragedies, but Sheffield Theatres themselves had only produced Euripides' *Iphigenia in Aulis* in 2003.
17. In a 2016 report by New Local Government Network and Arts Council England it was acknowledged that local authority investment in arts and culture had declined by 17% or £236 million between 2010 and 2015 (Harvey 9–11).
18. For information about the Olympic legacy prior to the event taking place, see Dabas. For analysis of the impact of the Cultural Olympiad, see Garcia and Cox.
19. For more on accent in Hall's *Oresteia*, see Latham as well as Marshall. While not explicitly stated in reference to *Prometheus Chained*, Tony Harrison has been an important influence on Henry Stead's work (Stead, 'Fire…' 212).

Works Cited

Billington, Michael. 'Sheffield's Crucible: The Revolutionary Theatre That Was almost Snookered.' *The Guardian*, 30 Nov. 2021, www.theguardian.com/stage/2021/nov/30/sheffield-crucible-revolutionary-theatre-snookered-colin-george. Accessed 19 Aug. 2023.

Bridges, Emma. 'Public Engagement with Classics Research in the UK: A Survey.' *CUCD Bulletin* 48 (2019): 1–25.

Bullen, David. 'Saving Classics with the *Clouds*: A Case Study in Adapting Aristophanes.' *Aristophanic Humour: Theory and Practice*, edited by Peter Swallow and Edith Hall, Bloomsbury, 2020, 205–214.

Culture, Media and Sport Committee. 'Funding of the Arts.' *Parliament.uk*, 22 Mar. 2011, www.publications.parliament.uk/pa/cm201011/cmselect/cmcumeds/464/46405.htm. Accessed 19 Aug. 2023.

Dabas, Laura. *The London 2012 Olympics and Lottery Funding: Impacts on Cultural Legacy in the UK*. Lap Lambert Academic Publishing, 2011.

Duncan, S., P. Manners, and K. Miller. *Reviewing Public Engagement in REF 2014: Reflections for Shaping the Second REF*. NCCPE, 2017.

Eastwood, David. *Circular Letter Number 06/2007*. 6 Mar. 2007. National Archives, https://webarchive.nationalarchives.gov.uk/ukgwa/20100303171159/http:/www.hefce.ac.uk/pubs/circlets/2007/cl06_07. Accessed 19 Aug. 2023.

Garcia, Beatriz, and Tamsin Cox. *London 2012 Cultural Olympiad Evaluation: Final Report*. Institute of Cultural Capital, 2013.

Hadley, Steven. *Audience Development and Cultural Policy*. Palgrave Macmillan, 2021.

Hall, Edith. 'The Promethean Politics of Education.' *The Edithorial*, 24 June 2012, www.edithorial.blogspot.com/2012/06/promethean-politics-of-education.html. Accessed 19 Aug. 2023.

———. *Tony Harrison: Poet of Radical Classicism*. Bloomsbury Academic, 2021.

Harrison, Tony. *The Trackers of Oxyrhynchus*. Faber and Faber, 1991.

Harvey, Adrian. *Funding Arts and Culture in a Time of Austerity*. New Local Government Network, 2016.

Hunt, Steven, and Arlene Holmes-Henderson. 'A Level Classics Poverty: Classical Subjects in Schools in England: Access, Attainment and Progression.' *CUCD Bulletin* 50 (2021): 1–26.

Latham, Caroline. 'The Sound of the *Oresteia*.' *Tony Harrison and the Classics*, edited by Sandie Byrne, Oxford University Press, 2022, 247–266.

Marshall, Hallie Rebecca. *Banging the Lyre: The Classical Plays of Tony Harrison*, Ph.D. Dissertation. University of British Columbia, 2009.

Orwell, George. *Road to Wigan Pier*. Gollancz, 1936.

Parkyn, Lottie. 'The Originality and Influence of Tony Harrison's *The Trackers of Oxyrhynchus*.' *Tony Harrison and the Classics*, edited by Sandie Byrne, Oxford University Press, 2022, 117–134.

REF2014. 'Research Excellence Framework 2014: Overview Report by Main Panel D and Sub-panels 27 to 36.' *Research Excellence Framework*, 2015, https://2014.ref.ac.uk/media/ref/content/expanel/member/Main%20Panel%20D%20overview%20report.pdf. Accessed 19 Aug. 2023.

Rogers, Megan. 'Actors of Dionysus.' *Journal of Classics Teaching* 20.40 (2019): 35–36.

Rokison-Woodall, Abigail. *Shakespeare in the Theatre: Nicholas Hytner*. Arden, 2017.

Sayer, Derek. *Rank Hypocrisies: The Insult of the REF*. SAGE Publications, 2014.

Sheffest. 2012, www.sheffest.wordpress.com. Accessed 19 Aug. 2023.

Shepherd, Jessica. 'Humanities Research Threatened by Demands for "Economic Impact".' *The Guardian*, 13 Oct. 2009, www.theguardian.com/education/2009/oct/13/research-funding-economic-impact-humanities. Accessed 19 Aug. 2023.

Shipton, Matthew. 'Why Prometheus?' *Sheffest*, 28 May 2012, www.sheffest.wordpress.com. Accessed 19 Aug. 2023.

Stead, Henry. 'Prometheus Chained—A Word from the Team.' *Sheffest*, 20 May 2012, www.sheffest.wordpress.com. Accessed 19 Aug. 2023.

———. 'Fire, Fennel, and the Future of Socialism.' *Tony Harrison and the Classics*, edited by Sandie Byrne, Oxford University Press, 2022, 202–221.

Stone, A. 'Cultural Olympiad Brings First International Student Drama Festival to Sheffield.' *University of Sheffield*, 18 June 2012.

Wiles, David. *Greek Theatre Performance: An Introduction*. Cambridge University Press, 2000.

Wilson, Nick, Jonathan Gross, and Anna Bull. *Towards Cultural Democracy*. King's College London, 2017.

9 Making Theatre Out of Fragments

Laura Swift

Tragic fragments are experiencing a renaissance. Until recently scholarship on fragmentary tragedies was largely confined to textual work or attempts to reconstruct the plots of lost plays.[1] The situation is very different from Greek lyric poetry, where even tiny fragments are analysed for literary and artistic significance. The difference of course is that for most of the lyric poets, there is no choice but to use fragments, and so scholars or students wanting to better understand Sappho or Simonides must grapple to extract meaning from a few tattered lines or words. Readers of tragedy interested in literary questions enjoy the luxury of 32 complete plays, so have paid little attention to how fragments might augment our knowledge of (say) the style of Euripides, or tragedy's depiction of gender roles. In recent years, however, there has been a growth of interest among tragedy specialists in the fragmentary plays, with several new editions and introductions.[2] These publications are by traditionally trained classicists whose motivation is to make the fragmentary plays accessible to a Greekless audience, and presuppose a readership who is interested in tragedy, though with little knowledge of texts that did not survive complete. At the same time, more interest is being paid to what fragmentary texts can tell scholars about the tragic genre, and how readers can approach them as literature, rather than purely pieces in a textual jigsaw puzzle.[3] Yet tragic fragments are not just texts but remnants of drama, meant for performance in front of an audience.[4] Fragmentation of text has been a strategy in what has been broadly termed the 'postdramatic', but these are plays fragmented through chance rather than by artistic choice. What, then, are the implications of approaching Greek tragedy—often claimed as the foundation of Western playwriting—through the performance of fragmentary remains rather than whole texts?[5] What can modern theatre practice teach us about how scholars can and should approach fragmented texts? How does performing fragmentary tragedies pull apart our certainties about Greek drama and its legacy in theatre history, by inviting us to reflect on what is canonical and why? This chapter will discuss my eight-year (and counting) collaboration with theatre makers, which seeks to answer these questions.

DOI: 10.4324/b22844-12

My own academic trajectory began in Greek tragedy before I moved to work on fragmentary lyric poetry. Re-entering tragedy studies from a sub-discipline where entire articles are devoted to a single surviving line, I was struck by the unmined riches in the so-called lost plays, and how they have the potential to make both audiences and scholars rethink what we know about the most familiar of ancient genres.[6] At the same time, these texts highlight the evocative power of the fragment, familiar to anyone who has fallen in love with the poems of Sappho.[7] Interest in classical fragments can be connected to wider historical and cultural moments: for example, the liking for classical ruins in the Romantic period,[8] or the coincidence of the thousands of papyri discovered in Egypt at the turn of the twentieth century with the growth of literary and artistic fragmentation in the modernist movement.[9] Yet the power fragments hold over the human mind long predates this, and does not appear to be culturally or temporally specific. For example, John Chapman's work on archaeological Fragmentation Theory suggests that interest in fragmentation is evident even in prehistoric times and recognises the role that incomplete objects play in creating social relationships and exploring our place in the world (Chapman). The appreciation of fragments, then, can be understood not as niche and technical, but rather as profoundly connected to our personhood and identity as human beings. Our project, titled *Fragments*, sought to explore Greek tragic fragments as drama, and to engage with the idea of fragmentation: its role in our lives, and why fragmenting information makes it so compelling.

Early Ideas

Fragments began life as a trial funded by the Being Human Festival and the AHRC, under a scheme entitled *Communicating Ancient Greece and Rome*. From its outset I have worked with Potential Difference, a theatre company that tells stories inspired by science, philosophy, and technology. The project has involved artists from a range of practices: deviser-performers, visual designers, puppeteers, a sound designer/composer, and a dramaturg and lyricist. The process has been a series of small performances and workshops, each building on the last and testing the underpinning of ideas from new perspectives. The first showing (then titled *Ancient Fragments*) was a kaleidoscope of ideas inspired by fragmentation, put together after two weeks of workshops and performed at Rich Mix in East London as part of the inaugural Being Human Festival in 2014. From that starting point the process was iterative: we devised, wrote, then tested what was written and tried new ways of devising around it. My role was not an academic consultant but an equal co-creator; similarly, the artists involved should be understood as co-researchers of the academic ideas. A more cohesive 'work in progress' show was performed at Ovalhouse in London and the Old Fire Station, Oxford in 2017. The ideas formulated were further developed through workshops in 2018 and crystallised towards a full production (originally due to take place in March 2020, but whose final development was delayed to April 2023 due to the pandemic). Each of these iterations had significant differences in tone, structure, and content, yet each built from surviving tragic fragments and the different ways people experience fragmentation.

As the project developed, we agreed on ground rules to underpin how we approached the concepts and texts. One was that the work should engage at a fundamental level with the experience of fragmentation. This placed practical limitations on how we dealt with the ancient text: the experience of being confronted with gaps was central, and we did not want to write faux-tragic dialogue to fill them. In particular, we set ourselves the rule that we would not invent new lines for characters who existed in the Euripidean play, though we were willing to rearrange Euripidean fragments to create new combinations, whether or not these seemed a plausible way to reconstruct the original text, if this served our dramatic aims. We were also happy to invent new characters whose dialogue need not be limited to original fragments. In order to guide the audience as to which parts of the text were Euripidean, the register of text written for new characters was colloquial, while the translations of the original retained a higher and more archaising tone, using heightened language and poetic phrasing and vocabulary (in the draft scripts, original fragments were in a different font, to help performers retain this distinction).

Early in the process, artists were invited to share ideas about what role fragmentation played in their daily lives. Their answers included visual fragmentation ('seeing snapsnots from a train', 'seeing part of a room through a window'), auditory ('hearing one side of a telephone conversation'), fragments as physical artefacts ('finding old letters or documents out of context'), but also the inherent fragmentation of human thought and memory ('partial memories of an event').[10] These 'common sense' experiences of fragmentation led to devised moments where fragmented image, sound, or dialogue was required. One outcome was a way of showing the curiosity fragments provoke. We discovered how unexpectedly compelling a mundane action becomes (washing hair, signing a letter, gesturing to someone) if staged such that only a small portion of the actor's body is visible. Just as the reader of a textual fragment is required to focus on the few details that survive, but cannot avoid the temptation to extrapolate about context, so too, these decontextualised fragments of action draw the spectator's attention to aspects of physicality that might otherwise be overlooked and provoke curiosity about the broader picture.

We initially experimented with different plays, but by the 2017 workshops, we settled on Euripides' *Cresphontes*. This was particularly suitable for two reasons. First, the surviving fragments are a good mixture of type and style. The play has several papyrus fragments, including a lengthy extract preserved on two overlapping papyri held in different collections (giving rise to discussions about how far to interrogate dramatically where fragments disagree). There are also smaller and more damaged papyri fragments, and a good number of 'book quotes' (lines preserved as quotations in the works of other authors), which are well preserved but devoid of context. Thus, in formal terms the play lent itself to varied approaches to ancient fragmentation. But just as importantly, its themes and plot spoke to the core ideas we aimed to explore.

Cresphontes is set in Messenia, the region of the Peloponnese which by Euripides' day was long enslaved by Sparta. The rough plot can be reconstructed by comparing it with the myth in Hyginus (*Fab.* 184b). It is a revenge play, which follows the youthful Cresphontes' return to his rightful kingdom from exile, as he seeks vengeance on his uncle Polyphontes, who murdered his father and older brothers and married his mother, Merope.[11] It is a play about misunderstanding, and the dangers of coming to conclusions based on imperfect knowledge. Polyphontes has put a bounty on Cresphontes' head, and the young man gains entry to the palace by pretending that he has killed the long-lost prince and has come to claim his reward. In the central scene, Merope attempts to kill Cresphontes in his sleep, believing him to be her son's murderer. It was reperformed regularly in antiquity and must have been a canonical text. Aristotle refers to it in his discussion of the 'best' tragic plot types (*Poetics* 1454a) and Plutarch discusses Merope's attempt to kill her son in terms which suggest his first- or second-century CE audience were familiar with the play in performance (*Mor.* 998e). Despite its fame, however, it was not included in the 'selection' that determined which tragic texts would survive into the modern era.[12] The plot has connections not only with the myth of the *Oresteia*, but also with other iconic non-classical legends (from *Hamlet* to Disney's *The Lion King*). This not only makes it accessible to a modern audience unfamiliar with Euripides (let alone his fragments) but also encourages them to reflect on story patterns and how we interpret the stories we tell through the lens of what we know and expect.

Piecing the World Together

To investigate the appeal of fragments, we turned to ideas derived from cognitive neuroscience, and the 2017 workshops were enriched through a collaboration with Professor Mark Stokes of Oxford University.[13] These sessions focused on how fragmentation is part of the human cognitive experience, and how the typical perception of a rich and detailed world is an illusion created by the brain's ability to fill in the gaps in sensory input based on what a person expects to be there. In fact, human brains are adept at converting a stream of (often low quality) fragments into what seems a coherent narrative. Thus, it transpires that perception is deeply connected to memory, since it is through our memories and experiences of what the world 'should' be like that we put together our perceptions of what it is like.[14] Nevertheless, there are limitations to this ability, which psychologists demonstrate to their students through various tricks or illusions. Once a pattern or expectation is established, it is difficult to 'unsee' what you have already seen. Well-known examples are change blindness or inattention blindness, phenomena that lead observers to overlook important aspects of the world around them or to be unable to notice changes in what they are looking at. For example, in the famous 'Harvard Basketball Experiment', viewers of a video are asked to count the passes made by one team, and while doing so, frequently fail to notice a person in a gorilla suit walking in and out of the match (Simons and Chabris). This reveals the brain's focus on certain aspects of sensory input and its inability to notice changes or details that do not fit with the desired narrative. During this section of the project, we also discussed the brain's dependence on occluders to create a 'logical' reason for fragmentation, and its desire to make sense of fragments by working them into a cohesive whole.[15]

There are clear methodological similarities between how we deal with fragmented information in our sensory perception, and how classicists (or theatre makers) handle a fragmented source. When an editor deals with a lacunose text, their responses take place on a more deliberative level than the unconscious alterations and assumptions a brain makes to fill in its surroundings. Nevertheless, approaching the issues as connected allows us to reflect more consciously on what it means to work with fragments, and the risks and benefits of the choices we might make. How far, for example, should an editor go down the path of filling in the gaps in order to make sense of the text? When should they choose to print a conjecture, either in the main text or in an apparatus criticus? How far is it possible to resist the pull of a particular interpretation once it has been suggested or made visible? How should the balance of responsibilities lie in terms of guiding the reader to understand, versus potentially leading them such that they struggle to 'unsee' the editor's personal interpretation? While editorial technique makes use of sigla such as square or angled brackets to make clear where text has been supplemented or removed by the editor, or dots to show which letters are uncertain, the unconscious impulse to create sense out of fragmentation gives great power to the act of putting something in print, regardless of how clearly it is marked as a modern editor's work. Moreover, the reader (or performer's) desire to read the work as complete creates a willingness to overlook traces of fragmentation even when they are put before them.

Once we accept the power a scholar's choices has over the unconscious assumptions of her later readers, we must also confront how these are rooted in individual personalities and experiences. Classics, like most traditional Humanities disciplines, has a discomfort with the personal voice, especially in sub-disciplines like philology or textual criticism, where it is felt that an argument should be universalisable and objectively valid.[16] Yet which reading one is drawn to is subjective, and editors' personalities define the choices they make (the conservative who sticks to the barest of facts; the cynic who constantly seeks to excise; the show-off keen to demonstrate their skill at verse composition). In a creative process, the academic and the personal cannot be separated, but our team's work on the text, combined with our growing interest in the neuroscience of fragments, brought me to reflect how far academic judgement depends not only on analytical rigour but on personal experience and mindset.[17]

During our workshops I found myself confronted with my own propensity to fill in gaps and construct a narrative beyond the evidence.[18] The longest surviving passage of *Cresphontes* is a section from the prologue (fr. 448a Kannicht), where the young hero in disguise asks another character questions about the royal house.[19] Eighteen lines of virtually complete dialogue survive, before the text becomes patchy. Like most tragic prologues, the purpose is largely to fill in the backstory for the audience, important for a myth that would be little known to Athenians.[20] The surviving Greek gives no indication as to the identity of Cresphontes' interlocutor (Character B). In what precedes the surviving lines, he or she must have said or done something to prompt Cresphontes' first line, which is to object to the master of the palace's attitude to strangers. Character B responds by contrasting him to the previous master (… 'the one who is no longer alive was most hospitable to all', 41).[21] This allows Cresphontes to ask questions about the dead king and his family.

Relatively far into our workshopping process, I realised that my interpretation of the scene was influenced by its similarities to the 'portress' scene in Euripides' *Helen* (437–482).[22] Here, Menelaus is shipwrecked in Egypt and refused entry to the palace by a (female) gatekeeper because of the master of the house's hatred of Greeks. While there are differences between the scenes (the *Helen* passage is laced with comic moments, while the *Cresphontes* seems serious; Menelaus really is a confused stranger while Cresphontes is dissembling), the thematic similarities are also clear (denial of hospitality, kingdom ruled by a suspicious tyrant, high-born visitor whose status is not obvious), and these led me to unconsciously assume that Cresphontes too was being refused entry to the palace by Character B. In fact, nothing proves that this is what prompts Cresphontes' question: he could, for example, be responding to a well-intentioned warning. Whereas the old woman in *Helen* aligns herself to her master Theoclymenus, and her attitude to Menelaus is hostile, Character B appears unsympathetic to Polyphontes, telling Cresphontes that 'he plotted in violence, so that he might rule the land' (49).[23] Rather than guarding access to the palace, Character B could be occupying quite a different role (for example, a maid loyal to Merope) and be drawn into conversation with Cresphontes while passing by.[24] The resulting discussion around this character and how much we can infer from the text and from tragic convention led us to develop a scene where Character B is repeatedly reinterpreted with different identities and attitudes, which become increasingly less Euripidean: we see the character as a gruff male gatekeeper, then in two rival incarnations of a maidservant, first terrified then manipulative and finally as a drunk weeping into his pint over the fate of Cresphontes' brothers. As the scene progresses, the changing identity of Character B also allows different 'logical' explanations for the increasing fragmentation of the dialogue (loud music in a bar, people going in and out of a door).

Putting this scene together led us to reflect on the role of parallels in classical scholarship to elucidate fragmentary texts. It is conventional when suggesting or critiquing a supplement, for example, to offer a parallel for the word's usage in that author, genre, or period. A lack of parallels is problematic; it means we have no assurance that this particular grammatical usage or meaning could be correct. On the other hand, the Greek that survives to generate parallels is a tiny fraction of the original evidence, so to insist too rigidly becomes reductive. In the case of tragic fragments, a search for parallels goes beyond word choices into broader questions of how we reconstruct action and characters (as with the prologue of *Cresphontes*, where *Helen* provides a parallel, whether useful or not). Scholars have a detailed knowledge of what is conventional in tragedy, and often use this to extrapolate what 'must' have happened in portions of a play they do not have. For example, we know tragic action is commonly set outside a palace and takes place within a single day. We know that violence and death take place off-stage and are described by a Messenger, that the gods may appear at the end of a play *ex machina* to offer resolution, and we know the plot types popular in tragic reworking of myths. Yet we also know that tragedy was a competitive genre, and so thrived on innovation and the overturning of expectations. Moreover, the selection process that determined which tragedies survived was not random but determined by pre-existing views as to what tragedy 'should' be.[25] Yet it is from the plays we have that we can conclude what is common, and our view on what is innovative depend only on it being rare in our small sample. If a different selection survived, we might claim that tragedy was 'always' set in one place, or that the Chorus 'always' remained on-stage once they had entered. As it is, scholars of tragedy assume that switching locations (as in *Eumenides* or *Ajax*) is possible but rare: if a further five plays with a scene change survived, one might conclude that it is a standard technique. Even for plays we have access to, our interpretation is based on assumptions about what is 'conventional', a narrowing of the genre which began with the literary criticism of Aristophanes and Aristotle in the 5th and 4th centuries BCE and their statements about what is characteristic. For example, in assessing the staging of Ajax's death in Sophocles' play, scholars who argue for the death taking place behind the *skēnē* strengthen their position by observing that there is no parallel for direct depiction of violence.[26] In *Cresphontes* itself, Collard, Cropp and Lee argue that Merope's attempt to kill the sleeping Cresphontes takes place off-stage (despite Plutarch's account of the fear it stirred in the audience) justifying their interpretation on the basis of parallels from Aeschylus' *Choephori* and Euripides' *Orestes*.[27] What then is the appropriate balance between creativity and rigour? How can we make evidence-based suggestions about a lost play without forcing ourselves into the position where (as a character in our 2017 script says) 'we just have to re-create the plays we already have, make everything exactly the same'?

Making Sense of the Gaps

Working with fragments, then, can be understood as speaking to a human experience which reaches far beyond the study of classical texts. A key question was how we could represent fragmentation theatrically, celebrating the gaps rather than filling them. One strategy was to depict scenes as interrupted or inaccessible. For example, the central scene in *Cresphontes*, now lost, consists of a meeting where Cresphontes convinces Polyphontes (and accidentally also his mother) that he has killed the missing prince and has come to claim the bounty. We experimented with staging this off-stage, visible only momentarily through a closing door, with the occasional word audible to an eavesdropper. Subsequently, the conflicting behaviour and memories of the characters depict their differing understanding of what took place in that room. Our 'rule' of not inventing new lines for Euripidean characters led to devising scenes where characters could not speak freely (for example fearing being overheard), and so conveyed meaning through body language and the occasional broken line. The consequence was that the 'main characters' became to an extent de-centred within their own narrative, with the audience's focus drawn increasingly to the marginalised (and invented) voices within the palace, a move which reflects a similar shift in the way scholars are now approaching the ancient world. We also experimented with visual and sound effects which create an experience of fragmentation, such as the use of 'phantom words' (a sequence of sounds that the listener can interpret as multiple different words),[28] or 'phonemic restoration' (snippets of sound that are meaningless until the silence is filled with white noise, which allows us to decode it).[29]

The final important strand was puppetry, which in its essence imposes meaning onto a fragmented piece of information. Puppetry capitalises on our brain's ability to load inanimate objects, including the simplest shapes, with stories and symbolism, if they are moved in a way that indicates they have a relationship with each other.[30] It also de-centres the body of the actor as the locus of meaning, and undermines the dominance of aesthetic realism which became central to twentieth- (and remains only less slightly central in twenty-first) century theatre. Shadow puppetry also allowed us to engage with the physical form of textual fragmentation: the papyrus scrap. The creative team visited the Oxyrhynchus Papyrus Collection in Oxford and the British Museum's conservation labs, in order to understand the process of curating and conserving papyri, and the techniques used to handle them. On stage, overhead projectors were repurposed to resemble the lightboxes used to examine papyri, which allowed the projection of shadow images onto the wall behind. As well as realistic images (such as measuring, brushing, or unfolding papyrus), the movement of papyrus on the OHP allowed us to build up images in pieces, for example, moving papyrus scraps in such a way as to suggest a figure or scene, which gives the audience the experience of their brains filling in gaps to create a narrative (see Figures 9.1 and 9.2).

Making Theatre Out of Fragments 121

Figure 9.1 In the 2017 Ovalhouse showing, performers experimented with using shapes on the OHP to represent 'realistic papyrology'. Artists: Bella Heesom and Tom Espiner. Photograph: Richard Wylie.

Figure 9.2 During puppetry workshops in 2020, the creative team experimented with moving and manipulating fragments of real (modern) papyri until finally the image of a king becomes clear. Photograph: Russell Bender.

Conclusion

What place, then, can fragmentary drama hold in the ecology of theatre or the practice of classical studies? For a start, the experience of working with fragments is a democratic one, which challenges deeply held assumptions about Classics, academia, and Greek theatre. From my perspective, working in a process that broke down traditional barriers between 'academic expert' and 'practitioner' allowed me to revisit assumptions about how expertise is created and shared, and what constitutes original research. More broadly, working on a 'lost' play forces us to reflect upon which literature is prized and which is discarded, and what lies behind those choices. As well as inviting us to confront assumptions about what makes 'great literature', it allows us to consider the alternative canons that could have shaped the tragic tradition if different choices had been made.

But a separate democratising force lay in the nature of fragments themselves. The strength of our impulse to fill in the gaps and piece fragments together was a constant challenge, due to an unresolvable tension between our choice to represent the experience of fragmentation, and the pressure to create coherence. Yet working with fragments offered great opportunities. Whereas fragmentary texts are usually seen as abstruse and difficult, beyond even the reach of most undergraduate classicists, their ability to speak to artists with no subject-specific knowledge suggests that fragmenting a text opens it up, by allowing a gap in which creativity can flourish. Finally, working on fragments allowed us to break down traditional barriers between Humanities and Science disciplines, by seeing the experience of dealing with fragmented information as something rooted in a shared humanity.

Notes

1 The vast majority of Greek tragedies do not survive in complete form. They are often referred to as 'lost plays', though sometimes small parts (fragments) are preserved, either through quotes in other authors or fragments of papyrus. Ancient plot summaries ('hypotheses') sometimes allow us to understand the broad outline.
2 For example, Wright, *Volume 1*, Wright, *Volume 2*, Cropp, 'Lost Tragedies', Collard and Cropp, Cropp, *Volume 1*, Cropp, *Volume 2*.
3 For example, Finglass and Coo. The first example of a substantial literary study of fragments is McHardy et al.
4 Much Greek literature was meant for performance rather than private reading, though tragedy remains unusual in still being consumed today largely through performance. On the importance of performance to classical reception, see Hall, though many performance theorists deny the validity of distinguishing between media and forms in this fashion: see Montgomery Griffiths, 192–204.
5 On the relationship of classical drama to the postdramatic, see Cole.
6 The fragments are collected in *Tragicorum Graecorum Fragmenta* (*TrGF*) and constitute five volumes. Many have been rarely studied: some have not even been translated.

Making Theatre Out of Fragments 123

7 As expressed in Rainer Maria Rilke's poem *Archaïscher Torso Apollos* (1908), on the artistic power of a broken statue.
8 For example, Shelley's *Laon and Cythna* (revised as *The Revolt of Islam*), where the Greek hero Laon interprets 'the broken tombs and columns riven' as 'dwellings of a race of mightier men' (754–759) and sees in them the potential of contemporary Greeks to liberate themselves from Ottoman rule (766–767).
9 Discussed in Goldschmidt, '"Orts, Scraps, and Fragments"' and in more detail Goldschmidt, *Fragmentary Modernism*.
10 Quotations are based on notes taken in workshops in 2014 and 2017.
11 The name of the murdered father was also Cresphontes, and references to him are preserved in the surviving fragments (the son is not named in what survives, but the title of the play indicates he was named after his father). To avoid confusion, we changed the name of the son in our play to Aeyptus, a name attested in other versions of the myth.
12 All the plays of Aeschylus and Sophocles (seven of each, including the probably inauthentic *Prometheus Bound*) and ten of the plays of Euripides survive through a process of canonisation which sought to identify the 'best' or 'most typical' work. The remaining eight Euripides tragedies (as well as his satyr play *Cyclops*) were preserved by the chance survival of part of a manuscript containing his works in alphabetical order (the surviving plays have titles beginning with Greek letters epsilon-kappa). It is no coincidence that these eight plays (the 'non-select') are more diverse in style and tone, and contain more 'non-tragic' elements such as patriotic celebration of Athens or romantic/humorous plots.
13 Mark Stokes passed away in January 2023 and we would like to acknowledge our great debt to him and appreciation for his generous insights. We are also grateful to the ESRC Impact Acceleration Account for funding this element of the project.
14 For experimental science on how a subject's expectations or memory can influence perception, see, e.g., Goldstone and Hinrichs, Kang et al.; on how context influences perception, see Bar.
15 The 'Bregman-Kanizsa illusion' demonstrates how it is easier to interpret fragments if an occluder is superimposed which makes sense of the missing parts, by depicting a group of fragmented letter "B"s and then the same series with an ink blot covering the gaps: Bregman, Kanizsa, Nakayama et al., Johnson and Olshausen.
16 Personal voice theory in Classics was explored in Hallett and Van Nortwick. Little further work has been done, though for a recent study see Goldhill. The situation is quite different in the discipline of theatre studies, where the personal voice is encouraged as a method of academic insight.
17 Cf. Ford Wiltshire, 171: 'My hunch, however, is that finally all of us—historians, scientists, social scientists, humanists alike—write out of who we are.'
18 For similar reflections on working with a classical text, see Rabinowitz and Bullen.
19 P. Oxy. 2458 (ed. Turner 1962) is a third-century CE papyrus containing lines 1–116 of the fragment; P. Mich. Inv. 6973 (edited by Bonnycastle and Koenen in the 1980s but finally published as Hsu, 'The Text of a Ptolemaic Fragment') is a second-century BCE papyrus which gives the text of lines 82–128. Line numberings are as in Collard et al.
20 There is no evidence for the myth before Euripides and none of the principal characters are found in independent sources. Euripides may have known a Messenian myth which does not otherwise find its way into the record. After Euripides we find references to the Cresphontes-myth in prose authors, who adapt it to suit the contemporary political context (conflict between Messenia and Sparta): e.g., Isoc. 6.22–3, 6.31, Pl. *Laws* 692b, Ephorus *FGrH* 70 F 116, Paus. 4.3.6–8. See Harder, 8–12.
21 ὁ δ' οὐκ ὢν πᾶσι προσφιλέστατος.
22 The similarities are noted by Hsu, 'An Interpretation of a Ptolemaic Fragment'.

23 βίαι δολώσας, ὡς τυραννεύοι χθονός.
24 This is suggested by Hsu, 'An Interpretation of a Ptolemaic Fragment'. In terms of how assumptions are built upon, it is notable that she first identifies the character as a maid tentatively and merely as a hypothetical (31), but the fact that the character is then referred to as 'the maid' for the rest of the article gives this identification greater weight in the mind of the reader.
25 Not least the views of Aristotle (*Poetics* 1452a–1453a).
26 For example, Finglass, *Sophocles*, 377 'There is no precedent for a violent death, or even severe wound, being inflicted on the fifth-century tragic (or even comic) stage'. See similarly Scullion, 96–97, Sommerstein, 45–55.
27 Collard et al., 146, though Harder, 114–117 argues that the audience must have directly experienced the scene.
28 See Deutsch, or for demonstrations of the technique her website at http://deutsch.ucsd.edu/psychology/pages.php?i=211
29 See Samuel.
30 Heider and Simmel is a classic psychology experiment demonstrating this. Participants were asked to watch a shadow display involving simple shapes (triangles and squares). Almost all interpreted it in terms of a narrative involving human beings.

Works Cited

Bar, Moshe. 'Visual Objects in Context.' *Nature Reviews Neuroscience* 5 (2004): 617–629.

Bregman, Albert S. 'Asking the "What For" Question in Auditory Perception.' *Perceptional Organization*, edited by Michael Kubovy and James R. Pomerantz, Erlbaum, 1981, 99–118.

Chapman, John. *Fragmentation in Archaeology. People, Places and Broken Objects in the Prehistory of South-Eastern Europe*. Routledge, 2000.

Collard, Christopher, et al. *Euripides: Selected Fragmentary Plays. Volume I*. Aris and Phillips, 1995.

Collard, Christopher and Martin Cropp. *Euripides: Fragments. Volume II*. Harvard University Press, 2008.

Cole, Emma. *Postdramatic Tragedies*. Oxford University Press, 2019.

Cropp, Martin. 'Lost Tragedies: A Survey.' *A Companion to Greek Tragedy*, edited by Justina Gregory, Wiley, 2005, 271–292.

———. *Minor Greek Tragedians, Volume 1: The Fifth Century. Fragments from the Tragedies with Selected Testimonia*. Liverpool University Press, 2019.

———. *Minor Greek Tragedians, Volume 2: Fourth Century and Hellenistic Poets*. Liverpool University Press, 2021.

Deutsch, Diana. *Musical Illusions and Phantom Words: How Music and Speech Unlock Mysteries of the Brain*. Oxford University Press, 2019.

Finglass, Patrick J. *Sophocles: Ajax*. Cambridge University Press, 2011.

Finglass, Patrick J., and Lyndsay Coo, editors. *Female Characters in Fragmentary Greek Tragedy*. Cambridge University Press, 2020.

Ford Wiltshire, Susan. 'The Authority of Experience.' *Compromising Traditions: The Personal Voice in Classical Scholarship*, edited by Judith P. Hallett and Thomas Van Nortwick, Routledge, 1996, 168–181.

Goldhill, Simon. *What Is a Jewish Classicist? Essays on the Personal Voice and Disciplinary Politics*. Bloomsbury, 2022.

Goldschmidt, Nora. '"Orts, Scraps, and Fragments": Translation, Non-Translation, and the Fragments of Ancient Greece.' *Modernism and Non-translation*, edited by Jason Harding and John Nash, Oxford University Press, 2019, 49–66.

———. *Fragmentary Modernism: The Classical Fragment in Literary and Visual Cultures c.1896–c.1936.* Oxford University Press, 2023.

Goldstone, David B., and James V. Hinrichs. 'Subjects' Expectations, Individual Variability, and the Scanning of Mental Images.' *Memory and Cognition* 13 (1985): 365–370.

Hall, Edith. 'Towards a Theory of Performance Reception.' *Arion* 12 (2004): 51–89.

Hallett, Judith P., and Thomas Van Nortwick, editors. *Compromising Traditions: The Personal Voice in Classical Scholarship.* Routledge, 1996.

Harder, Annette. *Euripides' Kresphontes and Archelaos.* Brill, 1985.

Heider, Fritz, and Marianne Simmel. 'An Experimental Study of Apparent Behavior.' *The American Journal of Psychology* 57 (1944): 243–259.

Hsu, Katherine. 'P. Mich. 6973: The Text of a Ptolemaic Fragment of Euripides' *Cresphontes.*' *ZPE* 190 (2014): 13–29.

———. 'P. Mich. 6973. An Interpretation of a Ptolemaic Fragment of Euripides' *Cresphontes.*' *ZPE* 190 (2014): 31–48.

Johnson, Jeffrey, and Bruno A. Olshausen. 'The Recognition of Partially Visible Natural Objects in the Presence and Absence of Their Occluders.' *Vision Research* 45 (2005): 3262–3276.

Kang, Min-Suk, et al. 'Visual Working Memory Contaminates Perception', *Psychonomic Bulletin Review* 18 (2011): 860–869.

Kanizsa, Gaetano. *Organization in Vision. Essays on Gestalt Perception.* Praeger, 1979.

McHardy, Fiona, et al., editors. *Lost Dramas of Classical Athens: Greek Tragic Fragments.* Liverpool University Press, 2005.

Montgomery Griffiths, Jane. 'Sappho, Performance, and Acting Fragments.' *A Companion to Greek Lyric*, edited by Laura Swift, Wiley, 2022, 192–204.

Nakayama, Ken, et al. 'Stereoscopic Depth: Its Relation to Image Segmentation, Grouping and the Recognition of Occluded Objects.' *Perception* 18 (1989): 55–68.

Rabinowitz, Nancy S., and David Bullen. '*Iphigenia in Tauris:* Iphigenia and Artemis? Reading Queer/Performing Queer.' *Queer Euripides: Re-Readings in Greek Tragedy*, edited by Sarah Olsen and Mario Teló, Bloomsbury, 2022, 197–206.

Samuel, Arthur. 'Phoneme Restoration.' *Language and Cognitive Processes* 11.6 (1996): 647–654.

Scullion, Scott. *Three Studies in Athenian Dramaturgy.* Teubner, 1994.

Simons, Daniel J., and Christopher F. Chabris. 'Gorillas in Our Midst: Sustained Inattentional Blindness for Dynamic Events.' *Perception* 28.9 (1999): 1059–1074.

Sommerstein, Alan H. 'Violence in Greek Drama.' *Ordia Prima* 3 (2004): 41–56.

Wright, Matthew. *The Lost Plays of Greek Tragedy: Volume 1. Neglected Authors.* Bloomsbury Academic, 2016.

———. *The Lost Plays of Greek Tragedy. Volume 2. Aeschylus, Sophocles and Euripides.* Bloomsbury Academic, 2018.

Index

Note: Page numbers in italics denote figures.

A level 6, 11, 14n11, 14n16, 38, 45, 50, 103
Academy of Live and Recorded Arts 37, 82n7
acting 31, 33, 35, 40n9, 48, 59, 64, 66, 72
actor(s) 12, 27, 31–36, 38–39, 43, 48, 50, 57–59, 61–65, 66n1, 67n7, 67n16, 67n18, 67n19, 80, 84, 86, 88, 90–91, 94, 108, 115, 120
Actors of Dionysus (aod) 12, 36–39, 40n9, 40n11, 47, 60, 103, 110n12, 110n13; artistic director 36
Actors' Studio, The (New York) 82n7
Aeschylus 11, 21, 123n12; *Agamemnon* 40n11, 42, 47, 72, 81n2; *Choephori* 119; *Eumenides* 119; *Oresteia* 21–22, 36, 108, 110n19, 116; *Persians* 40n11, 108; *Prometheus Bound* 72, 81n2, 102, 106–109, 110n6, 110n8, 110n19, 123n12; *Suppliants* (*The Suppliant Women*) 21, 94
agonism (*agon*) 61–66, 67n16, 78, 80
amateur 3, 13, 37, 43, 73, 89–91, 108
Archive of Performances of Greek and Roman Drama (APGRD) 12, 14n11, 28n3, 34–37, 39, 103–104; *Communicating Ancient Greece and Rome* scheme (CAGR) 101, 114
archive/s 33–35, 38, 40n5, 42, 44–46, 48
Aristophanes 119; *Birds* 49; *Clouds* 46; *Frogs* 47, 51, 72; *Lysistrata* 72; *Wasps* 47
Aristotle 14n18, 32, 119; *Poetics* 11, 65, 81n5, 116, 124n25
Arts Council England 107, 110n17

Athens 11, 61, 70, 78, 101, 108, 123n12
audience(s) 20, 24, 27, 32, 40n10, 42, 44–45, 47–50, 53n35, 62, 70–71, 73, 77–78, 80, 81n4, 87–89, 101, 103–106, 108, 113–116, 118–120, 124n27
authenticity 20, 27–28, 29n8, 48–49, 85, 93, 123n12
authority 24, 26–28, 34–35, 39, 61, 65

Barefaced Greek 73, 75, 77, 81n2
Barker, Harley Granville 20
BBC 6, 8, 14n13, 60
Billington, Michael 31
Boal, Augusto 37
By Jove Theatre Company 25, 47

(Royal) Central School of Speech and Drama 82n7
Chekhov, Michael 37
choreography 25, 61, 63, 75, 88, 91
chorus 12, 27, 40n9, 44, 48, 59–61, 63–66, 67n7, 67n17, 67n18, 70–82, 84, 86–88, 92, 94, 108, 119; community 12–13, 84–94, 108; flocking *see* Lecoq, Jacques
circus 37, 72
citizen(ship) 62, 66, 70–71, 77, 81n1, 82n5, 84, 86, 88, 94, 108
class 1, 14n8, 58; working-class 99
Classical Association (CA) 9–10, 38, 103
Classics for All 8–9, 14n15
'Classics poverty' 14n16, 40n8
climate crisis 52, 77
clowning 72

Index

Complicité 37, 59–60, 63; artistic director 59
comprehensive schools 102, 106, 110n4
consensus 12, 61–62, 66, 71, 78, 80
consultant 12, 19–25, 27–28, 114
(Royal) Court Theatre 20
Covid-19 pandemic 38, 50–52, 75, 77, 82n16, 115
Critical Ancient World Studies 2, 6–7
cultural democracy 13, 86, 94, 100, 109
Cultural Olympiad 107, 110n18

dance 27, 33, 67n7, 70–73, 76, 87
democracy 13, 62, 84, 87, 92, 94, 101
democratisation of culture 13, 86, 99, 109
director(s) 20, 22–27, 31, 33, 35, 39, 43, 46, 47, 49, 52n9, 70, 81, 82n8, 90, 104–105, 108, 110n14
Doerries, Bryan 108

East 15 82n7
École Philippe Gaulier 37
Euripides 11, 27, 113, 116, 123n12, 123n20; *Bacchae* 20, 22, 28n2, 33, 40n11, 46, 51; *Cresphontes* 115–116, 118–120; *Electra* 110n14; *Hecuba* 21; *Helen* 118–119; *Heracles* 44, 49, 53n32; *Hippolytus* 43, 49; *Iphigenia in Aulis* 110n16; *Iphigenia in Tauris* 50; *Medea* 14n11, 24, 40n11, 50, 52n1; *Orestes* 49, 119; *Phaethon* 73, 81n2

festival(s) 13, 45, 71, 99–100, 102–109, 110n8, 114
fragment(s): fragmentary texts 13, 51, 73, 113–124; *Fragments* 13, 24, 28, 28n6, 114
funding 2, 81, 102–105, 107

GCSE 38, 45, 50, 102
Goldhill, Simon 31–32, 34, 38
Greece 1, 7–8, 23, 34, 70, 73, 82n9, 82n14, 87, 100, 109
Greek Play (college/university): Bradfield College 53n14; Cambridge 43, 45, 49, 53n14, 72, 81n2, 82n6, 82n7; KCL 12, 42–52, 53n14; Oxford 42, 45, 49, 53n14; UCL 45, 53n14
Guildhall School of Music and Drama 106

Hall, Edith 21, 34, 101, 110n8
Hall, Peter 21, 105, 108
Harrison, Tony 21, 99, 108, 110n19
Haynes, Natalie 8–9, 14n13, 38
Higher Education 10, 12, 31, 57, 101, 110n8,
Hytner, Nicholas 105–106

improvisation(s) 62–63, 72
individualism 64, 78
Iris Project, The 103, 104, 110n12

Johnson, Boris 1, 8–9, 14n14
Julliard 82n7

King's College London (King's, KCL) 12, 42–52, 82n6

LAMDA (London Academy of Music and Dramatic Arts) 82n7
Lecoq, Jacques 12, 37, 58–67, 82n10; flocking 60, 73
liturgy 71
London 2, 43, 45, 47, 53n14, 58, 66n1, 103, 104, 105, 107, 108, 114

Macintosh, Fiona 34–36, 37
marketing 27, 38, 88, 90, 104
McCarthy, Lillah 20
meter 72–73
Mitchell, Katie 21, 22–23, 105
Mountview Academy of Theatre Arts 82n7
Murray, Gilbert 20, 26; the Gilbert Murray Trust 103

National Centre for Circus Arts 37
National Theatre (i.e. The Royal National Theatre of Great Britain) 6, 10, 21–23, 24, 27, 35, 105, 108; Artistic Director of 23, 105; National Theatre Live 110n13
neoliberalism 2

'Oxbridge' 1, 10, 14n16, 34
Oxford Research Centre of the Humanities (TORCH) 35, 36
Oxford School of Drama 37

participation 3, 10, 12, 44, 70–71, 72, 80–81, 81n4, 84–95
pedagogy 5, 12, 50, 52, 58–66, 66, 71, 73, 75, 80–81

playwright 11, 14n12, 19, 21, 22, 99, 104; playwriting 61, 114
Potential Difference 13, 24, 114
professional theatre 12, 24, 47, 84, 89–90, 92
public engagement 101–102, 110n10
puppetry, puppeteer 114, 120, *121*

Redgrave, Vanessa 32, 34
rehearsal, rehearsal room 12, 21–25, 35, 37, 52n10, 60, 72, 73, 75, 80, 82n6, 82n8, 88, 90–91, 93
Research Excellence Framework (REF) 46, 102
Rome 1, 7, 8, 14n14, 100, 101, 109, 110n2
Royal Holloway, University of London 36, 104, 110n8

Sappho 113, 114
secondary schools 100
Shasha, Tamsin 36–38, 39
Silk, Michael 45, 46–47, 49, 52n9
Singing 33, 70, 72–73, 78, 80, 86
Society for the Promotion of Hellenic Studies, The (SPHS) 103, 110n14
Sophocles 11, 123n12; *Ajax* 40n11, 46, 119; *Antigone* 5–6, 35, 40n11, 45, 50, 51, 72, 73, *74*, 81n2, 82n9, 103, 105, 108; *Electra* 21, 48; *Oedipus the King* 21, 50–51, 52n9, 75, *76*, 81n2; *The Thebans* 21
Stuttard, David 36–37, 38

Taplin, Oliver 21–24, 26, 34, 37
teaching 6, 8, 14n10, 28, 53n14, 60–61, 64–65, 70
Theater of War Productions 108
tradition 4, 5, 7–8, 39, 42–43, 46, 48–52, 57, 63, 67, 70, 73, 82n8, 82n9
training 26, 33, 37, 65, 72–73, 80–81, 82n8, 106; ancient choral training 70–71, 75, 81n1, 82n5; modern actor training 12, 35, 57–62, 64, 66n1
translation, translator 5–6, 19–24, 28n1

University College London (UCL) 45
University of Cambridge 8, 9–10, 27, 34, 43, 45, 49, 51, 72–73, 82n8, 105
University of Oxford 9–10, 12, 27, 34–36, 42, 45, 49, 51, 116, 120
university, universities 2, 5, 10, 19, 28, 42–43, 45–46, 50, 51, 59, 65, 101–102

West, Western 1, 7, 11, 14n15, 32, 87, 94, 100, 114
widening participation 100, 101, 109